The Last Three Feet

Case Studies in Public Diplomacy

2nd Edition

Edited by William P. Kiehl, EdD

The Last Three Feet: Case Studies in Public Diplomacy 2nd Edition

Published by The Public Diplomacy Council, Washington, DC

William P. Kiehl, EdD, Editor

ISBN-13: 978-1500865290

ISBN-10: 150086529X

Earlier Books in the Public Diplomacy Council Series

The Last Three Feet: Case Studies in Public Diplomacy
Edited by William P. Kiehl, 2012

Local Voices/Global Perspectives: Challenges Ahead for U.S. International Media
Edited by Alan L. Heil Jr., 2008

America's Dialogue with the World
Edited by William P. Kiehl, 2006

Engaging the Arab & Islamic Worlds through Public Diplomacy: A Report and Action Recommendations
Edited by William A. Rugh, 2004

This book is dedicated to all American and locally engaged staff who have conducted public diplomacy on behalf of the United States abroad. Your efforts have created mutual understanding and mutual respect, sparked creative dialogue, and led to many examples of positive change. You have made the world a better and a safer place.

It has always seemed to me that the real art in this business is not so much moving information or guidance or policy five or 10,000 miles. That is an electronic problem. The real art is to move it the last three feet in face-to-face conversation.

—Edward R. Murrow

Contents

Acknowledgments

M.E. "Bud" Jacobs, President, Public Diplomacy Council

The decade following the terror attacks of September 11, 2001, saw much heightened focus on how the United States and American people communicate with the rest of the world. Hearings were held, articles and editorials written, and studies were published by universities, think tanks, and the U.S. government. While many of these assessments raised important questions about U.S. public diplomacy, most failed to look at how public diplomacy actually works on the ground, the challenges public diplomacy officers and specialists face in conducting their duties, and the tools they employ to achieve their goals. Indeed, in the few instances where these issues were examined, the discussion was frequently ill-informed and most of the resulting conclusions and recommendations were not grounded in reality.

In part to address this shortfall, in November 2011 the Public Diplomacy Council joined with the Walter Roberts Foundation and George Washington University's Institute for Public Diplomacy and Global Communication to hold a forum, "The Last Three Feet: New Media, New Approaches, and New Challenges for American Public Diplomacy." The forum's title and main theme derived from an insight offered by the legendary Edward R. Murrow, who noted in 1963 that the art of public diplomacy "is to move it the last three feet in face-to-face conversation."

This book captures and expands the presentations offered at our forum. It is our hope that it will be a substantial contribution to the understanding of how things look in the "last three feet," especially in light of the changes technology and social media have made to the global communication environment. We believe that anyone interested in this subject—in government, the Congress, or academia—will find it a useful tool.

Many people contributed to the success of our forum and the publication of this book, and I thank them all. My personal gratitude goes to conference organizer Steve Chaplin and his team, professors Frank Sesno and Sean Aday at George Washington University, and Dr. Walter Roberts, who has guided and informed the efforts of literally thousands of public diplomacy practitioners, international broadcasters, students, researchers, and professors during his long and illustrious career. We are also very grateful to our editor, Dr. William Kiehl, for his energy and dedication in seeing this volume through to publication. Finally, I want to express my gratitude and high regard for our forum participants and contributors to this book. Without them, there would have been no forum or book. Indeed, without them and their colleagues in Washington and at posts around the world, there would be no effective public diplomacy.

1

Introduction
William P. Kiehl

In writing the introduction to this book I determined that it was important to let the reader know why this book should have been written in the first place and what the publication hoped to accomplish. These case studies on public diplomacy (PD) help to tell a largely unknown story about how American PD professionals go about their work in an overseas context. The goal is to provide a greater understanding of and appreciation for the art of public diplomacy and for the American and locally employed professionals who are in that "last three feet" at our embassies and consulates abroad.

The individual chapters will tell their own stories. Each of the case studies is quite different. A different writer with various talents, perceptions, and experiences presents each of the cases. Each of the writers, who are public diplomats, brings something special and unique to public diplomacy. Each of the countries selected for study, in their internal conditions and external relations, in their cultures and social systems, in all of this and more, emphasize differences. Yet, as we shall see, there are some common threads in public diplomacy that transcend the individual cases.

The concept of an elucidation of how public diplomacy actually functions abroad is something with which the Public Diplomacy Council, its individual members, and the PD community at large have wrestled. It is not an easy task for a public diplomat to talk about how she or he goes about the business of public diplomacy. As I wrote in an earlier work:

> Public diplomacy professionals are trained to stay out of the limelight themselves in order to utilize better the tools of public diplomacy to inform and persuade their audiences. They know that it is the message, not the messenger, that is the key. And to the extent that the messenger is someone other than an American diplomat or official, it is so much the better to provide credibility. Thus there is an "institutionalized reluctance" to speak about what one does. As the Wizard of Oz hastily shouted to Dorothy and her friends, "Pay no attention to that man behind the curtain!"

> [E]ven more so, the public diplomat, like so many other professionals, simply does not know how to explain his or her work to the layman. As Lisbeth B. Schorr wrote: "Even the best practitioners often can't give usable descriptions of what they do. Many successful [organizational and societal] interventions reflect the secret the fox confided to Saint-Exupery's Little Prince: What is essential is invisible to the eye. The practitioners know more than they can say."[1]

That is perhaps why so much of the history of American public diplomacy and nearly all of the analysis of the subject matter has been focused "inside the Beltway" rather than at overseas posts. That is why organizational changes and bureaucratic battles on interagency turf have overshadowed the actual work of public diplomacy. A great deal of ink has been spilled arguing the merits of various organizations or re-organizations of U.S. public diplomacy. Rather like a debate on the placement of deck chairs on the *Titanic*. Thus, when the public and their elected representatives think of public diplomacy—if they think of it at all—it is mainly in terms of the Washington bureaucracy and certainly not the work in the field. Indeed, the structure of public diplomacy has come in for more than its share of commentary, especially since the unwise amalgamation of USIA into the State Department in 1999. On this score, even this writer has contributed to a literature largely ignored by the greater public.[2] The latest example of this "inside baseball" tendency in discussions concerning public diplomacy is the *contretemps* over revisions of the Smith-Mundt Act of 1948, about which even some PD professionals know little and care less.

Field Operations—this little known and not well-understood aspect of public diplomacy—was something that the Public Diplomacy Council set about to bring to public attention. A working group of a dozen individuals devoted nearly a year to the planning and implementation of a one-day symposium to spotlight the work of public diplomacy in the field. Along the way, the "last three feet" statement by USIA Director Edward R. Murrow to a Congressional Committee in 1962 quoted in the front of this book seemed a most appropriate mantra for the symposium. The symposium, held in cooperation with The George Washington University's Institute on Public Diplomacy and Global Engagement and the Walter Roberts Endowment, took place on November 3, 2011. The planning committee realized, however, that as useful as the symposium was to showcase the work of public diplomats, its effect would be rather transitory. A more permanent and lasting vehicle to share this knowledge was needed. Thus, the symposium and the research that came as a direct result of it has enabled the creation of this book as a more lasting resource for scholars, students, and practitioners of public diplomacy worldwide.

The symposium acknowledged (and this book reaffirms) that the essential element missing from most discussions of public diplomacy is the role of public diplomacy as actually practiced abroad by American Foreign Service officers and locally employed staff. While the most visible PD resources are lodged in the Washington bureaucracy—the exchanges budget of the Bureau of Educational and Cultural Affairs, currently more than $600 million dollars, is a prime example—arguably the most important resources are found abroad in the cadre of public diplomacy professionals at embassies and consulates. This is in Edward R. Murrow's words, "the last three feet" of communication. Their day-to-day work, using local and Washington resources to inform, educate, influence, and persuade, is a story that should and will be told.

In the ever-growing public diplomacy literature, both academic and anecdotal, there remains a paltry representation of case studies of public diplomacy abroad. In reviewing the literature, very few examples stand out,[3] and none of these may be said to be *both* contemporary *and* written by a PD professional. That is, none until now.

This book fills an important gap in the literature in that it provides its readers with contemporary examples of overseas public diplomacy written by active PD professionals.

The following chapters and the interviews found in appendix 1 relate to every continent and represent a sizeable portion of the earth. One would have liked to have three or four times as many case studies in this volume, but time and resources did not permit a larger representation. We expect, however, that this book will inspire others to document their own case studies of public diplomacy and to add to the literature in the years to come.

Beatrice Camp, who served as Consul General in Shanghai during the period of the Shanghai World's Fair Expo, provides us with the inside story of this private–public partnership which snared an unexpected success out of the jaws of failure. Not every city can host a world's fair, but public–private partnerships are lessons that can serve many causes in many places.

The Arab Spring of 2011, with all its promise and uncertainty, is the backdrop for Rachel Graaf Leslie's examination of modern public diplomacy during a period of dramatic crisis in the Gulf. How a small diplomatic post in a volatile region coped with rapid social and political change has applicability in broader contexts.

Straddling Europe and the Islamic worlds, Turkey is seen as a key partner and the U.S. Embassy's public diplomacy section developed a number of innovative programs to reach Turkish audiences. Elizabeth McKay, who served as the cultural affairs officer during this period, addresses the process and the progress of these innovations.

Michael Anderson, a former public affairs officer in Indonesia, looks to the recent creation of a new kind of American "space" in Jakarta to provide a 21st century replacement for the American library and cultural center of the last century. Will @America be the future?

Exchanges, and especially youth exchanges, have played a vital role in American public diplomacy for 70 years or more. But exchanges don't just happen spontaneously. Jean Manes describes a state of the art model as developed in Brazil but which has applicability in many societies.

Social Media can play an important role in almost any country if developed and nurtured properly. In societies where face-to-face contact may be limited, that role becomes even more important, as Aaron Snipe describes in Baghdad. Putting a human face on social networking was an important step toward success.

Walter Douglas points out how important it is to pay attention to the other side of the dialogue. Especially in societies like Pakistan where the bilateral relationship is complicated, one needs to know precisely what our interlocutors are saying. Focusing on the authentic voices is most important.

Drawing on some of the skill sets described in these case studies, in the interviews and statements found in the appendices, and especially on his experiences in Africa, Bruce Wharton draws up a short list of the qualities essential for America's public diplomats now and in the future.

The four appendices themselves are important resources, including the interviews with PD professionals from around the world (Gloria Berbena, PAO Cuba; Ambassador John Beyrle, Russia; Atim Eneida George, PAO Nigeria; Gabriel Kaypaghian, PAO Mexico; Matt Lussenhop, PAO Afghanistan; Hayes Mahoney, PAO Egypt; Rakik Mansour, CAO France), Ambassador to Brazil Thomas Shannon's keynote address to the November 2011 symposium, and an exclusive interview with Olympic figure skater and Public Diplomacy Envoy Michele Kwan.

The publishers of this work hope that this book will be just a beginning: a beginning of a series of case studies on public diplomacy that will be written by the PD practitioners of today and tomorrow; a beginning of a more systematic study of and greater attention to the art of public diplomacy as practiced by PD professionals abroad; and a beginning of greater public awareness—and indeed greater public interest—in this important component of American foreign policy.

Notes

1. William P. Kiehl, "When the Rubber Meets The Road: PD As It Is Practiced Abroad," *Exchange: The Journal of Public Diplomacy*, Fall 2010, http://www.lulu.com/shop/association-of-public-diplomacy-scholars-syracuse-university/exchange-the-journal-of-public-diplomacy-inaugural-issue-fall-2010/paperback/product-12929579.html.
2. ———. "Addressing the Public Diplomacy Challenge," *Foreign Service Journal*, October 2009, http://www.pdworldwide.com/uploads/Addressing_the_Public_Diplomacy_Challenge.pdf.
3. William A. Rugh, ed. "The Practice of Public Diplomacy: Confronting Challenges Abroad." Palgrave McMillan, 2011; William P. Kiehl, "When the Rubber Meets the Road" op. cit.; Michael Canning, "The Overseas Post, The Forgotten Element of Our Public Diplomacy," Public Diplomacy Council, Dec. 1, 2008, http://www.publicdiplomacycouncil.org/sites/default/files/users/Lisa%20Retterath/canningoverseasposts.pdf.

2

How I Came to Love the Shanghai Expo

Beatrice Camp

Our Checkered Relationship with World's Fairs

Although the United States has its own glorious history of hosting world's fairs going back to the Philadelphia Centennial Exposition in 1876, we have had a spotty participation record in recent decades. Where once such international expositions were seen as prime sites to show off our country's achievements, today they hold little significance for the general American public.

The reasons are many, including post-Cold War disinterest in cultural diplomacy and legislation prohibiting the use of appropriated funding for an American presence at world's fairs unless expressly authorized by Congress. U.S. membership in the Bureau of International Expositions (BIE) ended in 2002 after Congress refused to provide funding for dues. With no world's fair hosted in the United States since 1984, many Americans have little clue as to what such an event can offer to either host cities or participating nations.

This set of circumstances creates huge obstacles for U.S. involvement in world's fairs today. We dropped out of the 2000 exposition in Hannover, Germany, and barely made it to the 2005 fair in Aichi, Japan. Many thought that China's invitation to build a U.S. pavilion at the 2010 Shanghai Expo was dead on arrival, even though the media and others predicted that a U.S. no-show at China's big party wouldn't go down well with the PRC government or public.

Fortunately, however, the combination of Chinese pressure and the pull of public diplomacy (PD) opportunities proved too strong to ignore—Shanghai Expo 2010 was an expo of necessity for the United States. After navigating a series of difficult challenges, the USA Pavilion at the Shanghai Expo opened on May 1, 2010, to the first of over 7 million Chinese visitors, who stood in line for hours to experience a bit of America. While the pavilion itself was a public-private partnership, our U.S. Consulate in Shanghai played a key role in moving the effort forward and exploiting the people-to-people diplomacy prospects that the event offered.

Background on Shanghai's Big Party

After winning the blessing of the BIE in 2001, the People's Republic of China spent the next decade planning the largest world's fair in history; the city of Shanghai aimed to take center stage in 2010 the way Beijing had done at the 2008 Olympics. The government of China sent invitation letters to over 190 countries and dozens more organizations, determined to draw more foreign nation participation than any previous expo. (China indeed succeeded in breaking this and many other world's fair records.)

In response to China's invitation, then-Secretary of State Condoleezza Rice signed a letter expressing U.S. interest and the Department's Bureau of Educational and Cultural Affairs (ECA) followed up with a request for proposals in October 2006. In early 2008, ECA selected a group to plan, design, raise money for, operate, and manage a USA pavilion at the Expo.

Navigating a Rough Road

After a year of stop-and-go progress that clouded the prospects for our participation, newly appointed Secretary of State Hillary Clinton in early 2009 recognized the importance of U.S. involvement in the Expo and set in motion fundraising that brought the USA Pavilion to life. By this time however, the basic design of the building and the contents were in place, with no chance for a competition or public comment. The fact that the pavilion organizers had hired a Canadian architect to design the building caused negative reaction. While the organizers' described the 6,000 square meter building as "an eagle spreading its wings in welcome," critics delighted in dubbing the building "a temporary NASA administrative building" or a "combination Bose Sound System/Air Purifier." While regretting the missed opportunity to showcase American architecture, my colleagues and I found some comfort in sharing our woes with other national pavilions that faced similar sarcasm, such as home front attacks on Australia's "rusting shed in Shanghai."

Journalists continued to question whether the authorized team would be able to raise the $60 million budgeted to build, equip, staff, manage, and dismantle the pavilion. If the money was not in the bank by a certain deadline, would the U.S. government be able to sign a participation contract with the Expo authorities? If the United States dropped out, what would happen to the prime real estate that had been saved for us near one of the main gates? Rumors circulated that a McDonald's would go up on the site if the American group could not mount a pavilion there.

While the Chinese media was consistently positive about the American effort, Western media focused on the potential negative consequences if the United States snubbed China by failing to take part. This story line was too juicy to ignore, with our only recourse continued expressions of confidence that the money would be raised and the pavilion built. The Western media quickly lost interest once our success was certain; one American reporter told me that his editor did not think readers would be interested in any stories about the Expo or the USA Pavilion in the absence of controversy.

Making it Happen

Other problems arose. The late start led to missed opportunities, while the corporate signage in the entrance area drew criticism from Americans who thought it was inappropriate for a national pavilion. In contrast, Chinese visitors were generally impressed by the corporate involvement; President Hu Jintao admired the sponsor wall during his visit to the pavilion. In addition, consulate and other Foreign Service officers had to tread carefully among the restrictions regarding fundraising and the use of appropriated funds; several of us were also the targets of online attacks by a small group of critics who seemed determined to see the project fail.

Even as we pressed forward, it was clear that the cumbersome process and late start required compromises in design and execution. I agreed with those who thought that the pavilion was too reliant on videos, even though I found the main show, a 4-D film titled *The Garden*, charming and effective. Several Chinese officials pointed to the lack of any pièce de résistance highlighting high technology, which is what many expected from a U.S. exhibit. Some Americans complained about insufficient attention being devoted to democracy, or education, or tourism promotion, issues that we were able to address in our programs during the course of the Expo. Those of us working at the consulate in Shanghai were frustrated by the slow hiring pace for the pavilion, which left our public affairs office fielding issues that should have been handled by private sector pavilion staff. We pushed for the early stand-up of a communications team that could explain the process and defuse the criticism.

Despite all these issues, we created a successful public–private partnership that presented public diplomacy on a massive scale and proved a bright spot in an otherwise testy year for U.S.–China relations. Ironically, some of our counterparts at other national pavilions told us they envied the ability of the USA Pavilion to raise private funds and work with private developers, rather than depend on a government bureaucracy. A number of countries reached out to pavilion and consulate staff to learn more about our public–private model both during and after the Expo. We shared our process, warts and all.

We raised over $60 million and built an entire organization and pavilion in roughly ten months, copied previous exhibition best practices such as the Student Ambassador Program, and took advantage of traditional PD tools such as performing arts and alumni programs. The Public Affairs Sections in Beijing and Shanghai provided continuous support throughout a long and ultimately successful effort that reached 7.3 million visitors directly and hundreds of millions more through media, social networking, and a virtual pavilion site.

Success on Multiple Levels

While I always believed that the United States would manage to be present at the Expo, I was surprised at just how broadly we were able to take advantage of our participation in the six-month extravaganza. President Hu Jintao came for a look, later followed by high-level leaders from every province of China and the central government. We welcomed visitors from 100 nations, the European Union, and the UN. The pavilion helped American states and municipalities promote investment and tourism as ten governors and twelve mayors brought delegations to the pavilion and hosted public events there. Other U.S. officials who came to the pavilion included Secretary Clinton, as well as three other Cabinet-level officials, and ten members of Congress. (For a full list of VIP visits and additional information about the pavilion, see the Commissioner General's final report at www.state.gov/documents/organization/160954.pdf.)

Former Secretary of State Madeleine Albright led a presidential delegation for our National Day celebration, which also featured entertainer Harry Connick Jr. and the University of Southern California Marching Band. Other American performers who took the stage at Expo ranged from Herbie Hancock and Didi Bridgewater to Ozomatli, Hawaiian hula dancers, a Texas cattle-roper, the U.S. Army's 25th Infantry Division marching band, the Chicago Bulls mascot, NBA stars, and *Sesame Street*'s Elmo.

Our 160 Mandarin-speaking U.S. student ambassadors represented 38 states and 84 universities. Their ability to welcome the crowds in fluent Mandarin (as well as Shanghainese and Cantonese) became one of the hallmarks of the USA Pavilion. With their youth and language skills, the student ambassadors joked with the crowds and encouraged audience response in a very American way; this was people-to-people diplomacy at its best. We were also proud that many of these young Americans took the Foreign Service exam at the consulate while in Shanghai; already a number are headed for careers dealing with U.S.–China issues. The student ambassadors met American VIP and government visitors as well, gaining career experience while the VIPs appreciated the hometown touch. When Chicago Mayor Richard Daley dedicated a statue by a Chicago artist on the Expo grounds, he did not miss the opportunity to take photos with students hailing from his city, all wearing Chicago t-shirts.

In addition, the pavilion and consulate staff organized more than one thousand cultural and entertainment programs featuring 150 different American groups, including four Grammy winners. The pavilion promoted American businesses and brands with 68 official sponsors and 16 official suppliers. Our presence generated more than 8,000 media stories in China, the United States and other nations. By going carbon-neutral, the pavilion helped live up to the environmental theme of the Expo. The pavilion also promoted interest in study in the United States: the University of Southern California reported in fall 2011 that applications from China had increased eightfold.

Shanghai high school and university students were invited to the USAP to exchange ideas with student ambassadors and learn about studying in the U.S. The U.S. student ambassadors came from 38 states and 89 universities, offering a broad range of experience as they chatted with Chinese visitors.

Telling America's Story

Welcoming as many as 50,000 visitors a day, the USA Pavilion provided an unprecedented opportunity to showcase American culture and values to the Chinese people. By the end of the Expo on October 31, 2010, the USA Pavilion had presented America's story and America's spirit to more than 7 million visitors. Many Chinese visitors were particularly struck by the video greetings of President Obama, who welcomed them to visit the United States. They watched attentively as the president noted that "we are bound by our common humanity and our shared curiosity. This includes the hopes we share with the people of China and the people around the world to work together to realize a healthy, sustainable, and prosperous future."

In the words of one middle-aged woman from Nanchang, "The more we learn about American culture, the more we appreciate it." One Chinese blogger went so far as to describe the USA Pavilion as a mirror that allows the Chinese to "see that the real shortage in China [as compared to the U.S.] is the spirit of humanism, public consciousness, solidarity, and cooperation."

While some visitors and officials said they expected more technology on display, the main 4-D movie made a deep impression on most Chinese visitors, who appreciated the message of teamwork, citizen involvement, and environmental awareness. The story told by *The Garden* was simple and compelling, showing a little girl who mobilized her community to turn an ugly vacant lot into a beautiful community garden. The movie's display of optimism, community spirit, and perseverance offered a metaphor both for the challenges of creating the pavilion and for the international community working together to achieve common goals and a better world.

Secretary Clinton's May 2010 visit was front page news.

Showcasing the United States in this way, instead of merely reinforcing the image of an economic and technological superpower, was one of the ways in which the USA Pavilion influenced Chinese perceptions of the United States. A survey by Fudan University of visitors exiting the pavilion reported increases in descriptions such as "friendly" and "culturally diverse" for the United States.

Eighty-six percent of those surveyed said they "agree with American values."

After the Expo, our public affairs office continued to distribute DVD copies of *The Garden* video. It remains available on Youku.com, one of China's largest online video sites, allowing millions more to experience the main themes of the USA Pavilion. We even sent copies to Kabul at the request of the wife of then-Ambassador to Afghanistan Karl Eikenberry, who was moved by the self-help, civil society message of the movie when she toured the pavilion with Afghani contacts.

In the end, the Shanghai Expo drew over 7.3 million visitors during May 1 through October 31, 2010. A record 189 countries participated in the Expo, along with 60 cities, corporations, and groups. American people-to-people diplomacy reached the biggest audiences I have seen in my career. Videos, exhibits, cultural programs, and American

---

Future Expos

Although the U.S. approach to participation in world's fairs remains ad hoc, our success in Shanghai was a factor in the decision by the U.S. Department of State East Asia and Pacific Affairs Bureau to push for a U.S. presence at the 2012 fair in Yeosu, Korea (http://www.worldexpo2012.com/). Those of us involved in the Shanghai Expo were pleased that some of the remaining funds from Shanghai became seed money to jump-start the U.S. pavilion in Korea. U.S. participation in the larger 2015 Milan Expo remains to be determined.

In the wake of the Shanghai Expo, our Consulate Expo Liaison Office prepared a report summarizing the lessons that we learned in an effort to benefit future Expo efforts. While every expo and every country is different, tasks such as coordinating with a private sector team or taking advantage of the PD opportunities are likely to be similar everywhere.

---

student guides at the pavilion offered 7.3 million visitors a face-to-face encounter with the United States. (The Smithsonian's popular National Air and Space Museum receives 7 million visitors a year, twice the period of the Expo.) For many millions of Chinese citizens, this was their first time to meet an American in person, an opportunity most of them would never have had if the United States had not joined in the Shanghai Expo 2010.

Two Narratives in the Land of the Two Seas

Rachel Graaf Leslie

Bahrain and the Public Diplomacy Climate

The Kingdom of Bahrain is a small archipelago in the Persian Gulf between Saudi Arabia and Iran. Its five inhabited islands are home to 1.2 million people, approximately 46 percent of whom are Bahrainis.[1] The country's small size—a land mass of only 295 sq. miles, roughly 3.5 times the size of Washington, DC—is disproportionate to its considerable influence on regional security and its status as a hub for banking and Islamic finance.

The religious and ethnic identity of Bahrain's Sunni and Shi'a populations play key roles, but its society is not divided into two monolithic sects. Indeed, within both the Sunni and Shi'a communities there are diverse religious views and political opinions. There are no recent publicly available statistics on the exact size of Sunni and Shi'a populations in the country. The latest census data on the percentages of Bahraini Sunni and Shi'a dates from 1941 and indicates that the percentage of Sunnis was 48 percent, while Shi'a comprised 52 percent of the population.[2] Unofficial estimates, which are highly contentious in

Bahrain, vary significantly, although several sources suggest that Shi'a make up approximately two-thirds of the Bahraini population.[3]

Historically Bahrain has been an open, politically moderate, and economically liberal Gulf state. American media most frequently note that Bahrain is the host of the U.S. Navy's Fifth Fleet; however, Bahrain's cooperation with the United States extends beyond that. The United States has maintained a longstanding, strong partnership with Bahrain's leadership and its people, beginning with the arrival of American missionaries over a century ago, followed by joint oil exploration in the 1930s, and the subsequent establishment of a U.S. Navy presence in 1949. More recently, Bahrain signed a free trade agreement with the United States that entered into force in 2006, and in 2008 Bahrain became the first Gulf country to lead Combined Task Force 152, a multinational Gulf Maritime Security coalition tasked with patrolling the strategic international waterways of the Persian Gulf. Additionally, Bahrain actively engages in counterterrorist finance activities and contributes to international counterterrorism operations.

Traditionally, Bahraini public opinion of the United States has been mixed. While some Bahrainis maintain a somewhat negative overall image of the United States and its policies, a significant percentage holds favorable opinions of American education, society and culture, science and technology, and the American people. Through its public diplomacy programming, the U.S. Embassy in Manama has developed relationships with a broad range of Bahrainis. Often individuals have been more receptive to the Embassy's programs and activities—for example, scholarships and exchange program opportunities—than its official messaging. The Embassy's public diplomacy strategy in the country sought to underscore how U.S. government policies and its diverse range of activities in Bahrain benefit the close relationship between the people of both countries.

2011 Social Unrest in Bahrain

While the 2011 unrest in Bahrain was often depicted in American and foreign media as primarily a religious clash between Sunni and Shi'a, in reality the struggle had less to do with Islamic religious differences between the two groups than with Shi'a perceptions of their continued exclusion from social, economic, and political structures by the ruling Sunni elite. Indeed, it is this perceived inequality between sects that has been the cause of low-level demonstrations and sometimes-violent uprisings in Bahrain for the past decade and a half.

During the past decade, the Government of Bahrain had undertaken a series of reforms to develop and diversify the country's economy and more fully utilize one of its most important resources: its human capital. Nevertheless, many Shi'a viewed the actual application of these reform policies as being anything but even-handed. Many Shi'a claim that they face discrimination when applying for government jobs in key agencies such as the Ministry of Interior and Bahrain Defense Force, and allege that the regime harbors suspicions about their loyalties. Equally, many Shi'a contend that they are offered far fewer economic opportunities, that they are discriminated against with regard to public services and social programs, and that their poverty levels are much higher than those of their Sunni counterparts. Many Sunnis contest these claims, asserting not only that there are many affluent Shi'a families in Bahrain with successful businesses, but that many Sunnis also must contend with economic disenfranchisement.

Bahraini Shi'a also point to a number of political grievances, and they chose the date of the initial widespread protests—February 14—precisely for its political symbolism. February 14, 2011, was the 10-year anniversary of the adoption of the country's National Action Charter, which both Sunni and Shi'a almost uniformly supported in a 2001 referendum.[4] The National Action Charter paved the way for wide-ranging reforms spearheaded by King Hamad bin Isa Al Khalifa, including loosening restrictive state security laws, granting amnesty to political prisoners, conducting parliamentary elections (the first since the dissolution of the country's National Assembly in 1975), and the drafting of a new constitution. For opponents of the Bahraini regime, it is the latter that came to symbolize a false promise of political reform. Not only do they allege that the 2002 constitution promulgated on February 14, 2002, lacked popular support, they also maintain that the country's legislative body does not provide for equitable political representation.[5]

While perceptions of exclusion and political and economic discontent initially fueled the core of the spring 2011 unrest, in the months following, the clashes between Sunni and Shi'a Bahrainis assumed an increasingly religious cast. For example, Sunnis began openly referring to their Shi'a counterparts as "sons of *mut'a*" (short-term marriages deemed permissible by some Shi'a and which many Sunnis contend are unlawful and akin to prostitution), and "*rawafidh*" (a derogatory slur indicating that Shi'a reject the Companions of the Prophet Mohammed), while Shi'a overtly called the Sunni names like "*Yazidi*" (a reference to the second Caliph of the Umayyad [Sunni] Caliphate, who many Shi'a contend was morally corrupt and guilty of debauchery, the rape of women and children, wine-drinking, and other offenses). During the course of events in spring 2011, Bahrain's Sunni and Shi'a traded insults and made broad generalizations about each other's opinions and allegiances based on their respective backgrounds and origins. Given its small population, rarely is there a Bahraini who is not known in person, by family name, by social status, and often by religious beliefs. Indeed, it is quite common for Bahrainis to be able to discern from an individual's name their family group, the social categories to which they belong, the origin of their settlement in the country, and their marriage patterns, occupations, and educational achievements.[6] During the unrest in 2011, inaccurate assumptions about the affiliations and loyalties of Bahrainis resulted in devastating consequences.

Key Developments in Bahrain during Spring 2011

Beginning in late January 2011, the February 14th Movement, a loosely and virtually connected group, organized a "Day of Wrath" and called for demonstrations of youth and adults on February 14 at the Pearl Roundabout (colloquially known as the "Lulu"), a well-known monument that would later become an icon for many Shi'a, symbolizing their collective struggle for political, economic, and social reform in Bahrain.[7] On February 14 and during the following several days there were demonstrations throughout Bahrain. The largest of which was at the Pearl Roundabout, where several thousand protesters gathered and clashed with security forces. Two protesters were fatally shot in the countrywide demonstrations. Tension continued to build in Bahrain, and the number of protesters at the Pearl Roundabout swelled. On February 17, the government ordered the Bahraini police to regain control of the Pearl Roundabout and clear the area of all demonstrators, many of whom had spent the night there in tents. The clashes resulted in injuries of both policemen and demonstrators, as well as the deaths of several protesters. Confrontations and violence continued throughout Bahrain, in large part sparked by the anger over the crackdown at the Pearl Roundabout.

Bahraini security forces withdrew from the Pearl Roundabout on February 19 on orders of King Hamad, and protesters returned to occupy the space. Over the following weeks, the number of protesters would swell at times to more than 150,000 people.[8] In the weeks following the first clearing of the Pearl Roundabout, there were widespread strikes and demonstrations organized by both public and private sector employees; continuing demonstrations at prominent locations such as Salmaniya Medical Complex, the University of Bahrain, several government ministries, and public schools; numerous demonstrations and sectarian clashes in both Sunni and Shi'a neighborhoods; assaults on individuals and vandalism of private property; and the establishment of unofficial checkpoints by gangs of armed vigilantes who patrolled neighborhoods and villages.

By the end of February, the protesters' demands started to shift. Instead of advocating changes to Bahrain's constitution, increased authority for the lower house of parliament, and greater economic and social parity between Sunni and Shi'a, they began calling for the abdication of the regime and establishment of a constitutional monarchy. By early March, the protests at the Pearl Roundabout had metastasized and spread to the Financial Harbor of Bahrain, a key nearby financial and business district, and demonstrators began obstructing traffic in the area. By mid-March, the level of security and law and order in Bahrain had deteriorated considerably.

On March 14, Saudi military forces, part of the Gulf Cooperation Council (GCC) Shield Forces, rolled across the 15.5-mile causeway separating Saudi Arabia and Bahrain. The following day, King Hamad declared a three-month

State of National Safety that would later lead to curfews in limited areas and official checkpoints throughout the country. Most notably, the Bahraini regime decided to clear the Pearl Roundabout, Financial Harbor, and Salmaniya Medical Complex of protesters beginning in the early morning hours of March 16. In these and in other locations throughout the country, Bahraini security forces clashed with protesters, resulting in several deaths and numerous injuries. Following the second clearing of the Pearl Roundabout, the government began arresting opposition leaders, and later detained and questioned individuals who participated in or were suspected of participating in protests at the Pearl Roundabout, Financial Harbor, and Salmanyia Medical Complex, among others. There were also innumerable reports of individuals who were detained, arrested, or harassed at checkpoints as a result of their religious affiliation. Although some semblance of order and normalcy returned to Bahrain by March 21, with some businesses reopening and some students returning to schools, scattered demonstrations and protester clashes with Bahraini security forces continued in villages throughout the country.

The Media Environment during the Country's Unrest

Understanding how the media climate in Bahrain changed in the wake of the demonstrations requires some familiarity with the press environment prior to the spring of 2011. Seven independent daily newspapers operate in Bahrain: five in Arabic, and two in English. While most of the newspapers are perceived to be pro-government to varying degrees, only one of the Arabic dailies, *Al-Wasat*, is considered to be a "Shi'a opposition" newspaper. As in most Arab countries, satellite channels abound in Bahrain. The primary local Arabic television channel, known as Bahrain TV (BTV), is owned and operated by the

Government of Bahrain, as are all of the local radio stations and the Bahrain News Agency.[9] Although the Bahraini press law of 2002 provided unprecedented freedoms for local journalists, allowing them to openly express opinions regarding domestic political and social issues (within limits), most newspapers practice self-censorship. The Information Affairs Authority, Bahrain's information ministry, exercises oversight over all print and electronic media and occasionally censured print media and blocked Web sites prior to the 2011 unrest.

There were two notable waves of change in the media environment in Bahrain during the spring and summer of 2011. During the first wave, youth and adult activists used social media and mobile phone text messaging to unprecedented degrees, namely to organize widespread and sustained demonstrations that attracted thousands of participants. Additionally, it was a unique period in which the local press openly discussed issues of sectarianism. Most importantly, the demonstrations on February 14 and the events that followed continuously put Bahrain in the international media spotlight. During the second wave, social media use by Bahraini citizens, political groups, and the government proliferated exponentially. Unfortunately, a considerable amount of social media content increased the sectarian divide in the country, and conventional media was similarly polarizing. Furthermore, foreign journalists began to experience challenges entering Bahrain to report current events.

The First Wave of Change

The first wave occurred from February until mid-March. The February 14th Movement, which took its cues from the Arab Spring revolutions in Tunisia and Egypt, initially materialized online and primarily used social media and text messaging to organize protests. As the February 14 date neared, the Movement's Facebook and Twitter pages amassed tens of thousands of followers seemingly overnight. Although Bahrainis' recreational use of social media had been steadily growing over the past couple of years—for example, in December 2010, approximately 22 percent of the total population was using Facebook[10]—the Movement's call for protests in mid-February marked an upswing in the use of social media for political and social activism. Furthermore, the fast-changing events in Bahrain beginning in mid-February resulted in an uptick in the quick dissemination of information (or misinformation) via social media.

Also during this first wave, there was a notable change in the Bahraini regime's treatment of the sectarianism that had been brewing for years. Following the deaths of two protesters as a result of clashes with Bahrain's security forces, King Hamad offered a rare televised address on BTV on February 15 in which he acknowledged the deaths of the protesters, expressed his condolences, called for an investigation, and reaffirmed his commitment to reforms. Nevertheless, tensions continued unabated, and following the first clearing of the Pearl Roundabout, Crown Prince Salman bin Hamad Al Khalifa gave a hastily arranged national address on BTV on February 18 in which he expressed condolences for the events at the Pearl Roundabout, called for restraint by Bahrain's security forces, and invited Bahrainis of all backgrounds to dialogue.

The televised speeches by King Hamad and Crown Prince Salman were significant. In recent memory, the official media had never covered nor acknowledged the demonstrations or clashes between protesters and security forces that had been taking place in Bahrain for years. The speeches gave tacit approval for Bahraini media outlets to more frankly discuss recent political events and thus the floodgates opened—at least for a short while. Several pro-government newspapers ran articles about the clashes and the word "sectarianism" was bandied about in publications more frequently than it had been in previous years. BTV began interviewing protesters at the Pearl Roundabout, who had again occupied the space following the Crown Prince's speech. This alone was a newsworthy "first": BTV had never discussed sectarian tensions in the country, had never acknowledged protestors' demands, and had rarely (if ever) reported live from venues outside of its studios.

Given the concurrent Arab Spring revolutions in Egypt and Tunisia, it was not surprising that the protests in Bahrain received significant foreign media attention. What is interesting is that both Sunni and Shi'a groups heavily criticized the press coverage that Bahrain received. The National Unity Gathering, a predominantly Sunni political group founded in February, expressed discontent that media coverage by foreign correspondents focused more exclusively on the Pearl Roundabout and less on the pro-government protests and rallies occurring throughout the country. Conversely, many demonstrators at the Pearl Roundabout and elsewhere criticized BTV—despite its unprecedented coverage of protests—for biased reporting of events in the country and for inciting sectarian tension. On March 4 and March 9, demonstrators gathered at the Information Affairs Authority to protest coverage by BTV that they claimed did not acknowledge the government's human rights violations against protesters.

The Second Wave of Change
The second wave of change in the media in Bahrain occurred from mid-March, when there was an enormous spike in the use of social media to communicate, object to events in the country, rally like-minded individuals, and try to keep abreast of the quickly-changing situation in local

neighborhoods. Bahraini blogs that previously attracted 600 daily readers suddenly increased to over 3,000 readers. According to social media statistics, the growth rate of Facebook users in Bahrain from February 14 to April 5, 2011, increased by 15 percent as compared with 6 percent during the same time period in 2010.[11] Additionally, by March 30, 2011, there were roughly 62,000 active Twitter users in Bahrain—the second highest in the Gulf region—who generated 1,350,000 tweets (or messages) between January and March.[12] Seemingly everyone in Bahrain was online and had something to say.

It was not solely Bahraini citizens who were experimenting with social media as communications platforms. Bahraini government ministries such as the Ministry of Interior established Twitter accounts to try to get ahead of conventional or social media reporting cycles and counter what they considered to be sensationalist allegations about its security measures. Bahrain News Agency, the official mouthpiece of the Government of Bahrain, revamped both its English and Arabic Web sites, making them more interactive and user-friendly. Furthermore, the largest Shi'a opposition political society in Bahrain, Al-Wefaq, capitalized on digital and social media to organize subsequent demonstrations, conduct press outreach to foreign media outlets, and mobilize domestic and international supporters.

Not all of the increases in social media use were benign. Both opposition and pro-government Bahrainis used social media to advance their agendas by exaggerating events on the ground, disseminating inaccurate information, issuing threats, naming and shaming individuals, and spreading malicious propaganda, all of which increased sectarian tensions. Two "Lists of Shame"—one slandering Bahraini pro-government journalists and the other defaming "opposition" journalists—were disseminated on blogs and social media sites. Moreover, several social media posts displayed photos and malicious commentary accusing Bahrainis of all stripes of participating in protests and requesting information about their identity. Given the relatively small population in Bahrain, such actions reverberated broadly throughout the country.

BTV was equally polarizing, evolving into an echo chamber for angry individuals (predominantly Sunni) with an anti-Shi'a bent. One of BTV's live programs, *Al-Rased*, broadcasted hours of vitriolic commentary about opposition political leaders, journalists, doctors, academics, human rights activists, and citizens who participated in demonstrations at the Pearl Roundabout in February and March. BTV also displayed photos of protesters and questioned their loyalty to Bahrain, insinuating that they had links to Iran by nature of their religious affiliation. Bahraini Shi'a commonly believed that if one was mentioned on *Al-Rased* or a similar program, that they would be arrested and questioned shortly thereafter.[13]

Pan-Arab satellite TV channels also joined the fray. Hardline Sunni stations such as *Al-Wasal* broadcasted rants by Bahraini Sunni about their Shi'a counterparts, particularly Bahraini opposition leaders. Similarly, breathless reporting by Iranian-controlled *Al-Alam* and *Press TV* about Sunni offenses against Bahraini Shi'a exacerbated sectarian tensions. The slanderous and scathing commentary and YouTube video clips from the pan-Arab stations often spilled over into the social media realm in Bahrain and intensified the sectarian divide.

The second wave of media change negatively affected conventional and social media journalists. Several Bahraini bloggers were arrested, likely as a result of their online commentary. Beginning in February 2011, the Government of Bahrain began to more robustly enforce its visa policy for journalists: several foreign correspondents were denied visas at the airport, detained at the airport for extended periods of time before being expatriated, or had their equipment confiscated. The government also expelled a Reuters journalist who had been resident in Bahrain for several years. In 2011, Bahrain was added to Reporters Without Borders' list of "Countries of Surveillance" for Internet freedom, and many Bahrainis alleged that the regime increased measures to monitor and control Internet sites, as well as to punish those who spoke ill of the regime in online forums.[14] Additionally, in Reporters Without Borders' worldwide 2011–2012 Press Freedom Index, Bahrain fell 29 places to 173 out of 179.[15]

Challenges to Media Outreach in Bahrain

If you didn't see it with your own eyes or hear it with your own ears, don't invent it with your small mind and share it with your big mouth.

—Facebook status posting

The quote above, posted on the Facebook wall of an Egyptian-American in the midst of the revolution in Egypt, also fittingly summarizes the challenges of conveying the U.S. government's message to Bahraini audiences during the spring 2011 unrest. While trying to conduct press outreach, the Embassy faced a cacophony of voices, a multiplicity of narratives, and the proliferation of misinformation about the U.S. position and intentions.

From February onward, the rapidly shifting landscape in Bahrain resulted in an overwhelming volume of information circulating on social media and traditional media outlets. The fluidity of the situation on the ground and the massive amount of information online made it challenging to monitor Bahraini media and amplify the U.S. government's message. One of the biggest implications of this new press environment was that the U.S. Embassy in Manama first learned of events and, in some instances, even official statements by the Government of Bahrain from Facebook postings or Twitter messages. For example, through social media, the Embassy became aware of clashes and casualties at Salmaniya Medical Complex, of protests in Sunni areas throughout the country and at the University of Bahrain, and of the disappearances and arrests of Bahraini bloggers. Monitoring social media, blogs, and official Bahraini government Web sites required more than just the Public Affairs Section; it called for a coordinated effort among several Embassy sections to establish a clear picture of what was going on in the country.

Moreover, the Embassy faced the challenge of how to interpret the overwhelming amount of information—or more often, misinformation—that was being disseminated about the situation in Bahrain. For much of 2011, officials at the State Department and in the interagency closely followed the events in Bahrain, and it was the Embassy's job to separate fact from fiction and ensure that Washington had an accurate understanding of events on the ground. Embassy staff invested considerable effort following up on the false reporting that for a short time became the prevailing narrative on the island. Inaccurate stories spread quickly via social media, including erroneous accounts of the deaths of children caught in the unrest; the resignation of ministers who had not left their posts; the arrests of political activists who had not been incarcerated; unsubstantiated rumors of the rape and death of an incarcerated young poet; and even the fabricated report that Crown Prince Salman had been placed under house arrest. Additionally, the proliferation of social media resulted in voluminous amounts of photos and video clips being shared via e-mail, smart phones, and social media sites. In several instances, gruesome photos allegedly depicting current events in Bahrain had actually been taken months or even years earlier in locations outside of Bahrain. Furthermore, it was not simply social media stories that required substantial pushback; hastily filed news stories by foreign correspondents also distorted facts on the ground, such as the account that Bahraini military helicopters were firing on protesters.[16] It was the Embassy's role to research and drill down to develop an accurate understanding of what was really happening in Bahrain.

The Embassy also needed to engage proactively in press outreach to amplify the U.S. government's position on the situation in Bahrain. It was imperative that in doing so, the Embassy strike a delicate balance among all parties by concurrently promoting respect for universal human rights, affirming the importance of the U.S.–Bahraini relationship, emphasizing the U.S. government's strong commitment to the people and government of Bahrain, and encouraging dialogue among all groups in Bahrain. Although the Embassy treaded carefully with regard to its public posture, sometimes these efforts at balance were more successful than others.

Before the unrest, the Embassy's public affairs section normally relied on traditional media outlets to help disseminate the U.S. message. Beginning in April 2011, during the second wave of media change, this became much more difficult to do since several pro-government newspapers (whose readership was predominantly Sunni) published a series of articles and editorials insinuating that the United States was behind the unrest in Bahrain. In these articles, the Embassy was blamed for providing "false and politicized reports and information" to colleagues in the

U.S. government, which had allegedly distorted Bahrain's image in Washington. Similarly, the Embassy was accused of "interference" in Bahraini political affairs and criticized for its contact with Shi'a opposition groups that were "supported by Iran and Hezbollah." A columnist for *Al-Watan* leveled an ongoing campaign against the Embassy in which he asserted that the United States sought allies in Bahrain who are "supporters of an Iranian-style theocratic government," thereby incorrectly implying that the United States was attempting to change the political scene in Bahrain and establish a Shi'a theocracy.

Although the Embassy routinely disseminated numerous White House and Department of State press statements expressing the U.S. government's position on the situation in Bahrain, all sides selectively cherry-picked from these statements, with each reporting only the most desirable sound bites that fit their agenda. For example, whereas the Bahrain News Agency prominently highlighted Secretary Clinton's statements in mid-March that Bahrain was entitled to call on its GCC counterparts for [security] assistance, it ignored her statements in an interview in which she noted that Bahrain was "on the wrong track." Similarly, with the exception of *Al-Wasat* newspaper, Bahraini media ignored references to imprisoned Bahraini opposition leaders and the demolition of Shi'a places of worship in President Obama's May 19 speech on U.S. policy in the Middle East and North Africa. As a third example, following a June 16 press conference in Bahrain by Assistant Secretary of State for Democracy, Human Rights, and Labor Michael Posner, two pro-government newspapers erroneously claimed that the assistant secretary characterized the Bahraini judiciary as "fair" and "independent."[17] For a number of months, Bahrainis on all sides were only privy to half of the story about U.S. policies.

To counter the selective reporting in Bahrain's traditional media, the public affairs section began using digital and social media to disseminate full, unedited versions of U.S. government statements. In addition to sending statements via e-mail to key contacts and posting information on the Embassy's Web site, the public affairs section also relied on the Embassy Facebook page. As a result of the shifting media climate, the public affairs section also created an Embassy Twitter account to disseminate statements in Arabic and English. Additionally, the section recorded and posted content for the Embassy's YouTube channel, such as the Assistant Secretary Posner's press conference. In this way, the Embassy was able to more effectively inform Bahrainis of the U.S. position, which was generally more balanced than was being reported in the local media.

That said, the increased use of digital and social media by the public affairs section created unanticipated challenges. From February to April, many Sunni and Shi'a Facebook users used the Embassy's Facebook page to conduct a proxy war of words, posting poisonous sectarian commentary. This was an unexpected development; prior to February 2011, most of the Embassy's Facebook interactions dealt with public diplomacy programs or educational advising instead of political commentary. Beginning in February, however, most visitors to the Embassy's Facebook page were constantly demanding information on the U.S. position on the situation in Bahrain. In order to cope with the onslaught of insulting and sectarian remarks, grisly photos, and inappropriate commentary, the public affairs section temporarily limited the content that could be posted to its Facebook wall and prominently featured a strongly worded "terms of use" statement on the Embassy page. It also blocked a handful of users from posting on the Embassy's Facebook page after they consistently violated those terms. To the largest extent possible, the Embassy engaged in the conversation that was occurring in Bahrain via social media, although its messages were sometimes buried under the avalanche of responses it received whenever it posted something to social media sites.

Another interesting and unexpected occurrence was the response from American citizens living in Bahrain who followed the Embassy's Facebook interactions. The public affairs section received a number of complaints from individuals who firmly believed that the Embassy's Facebook page should be used solely as a means of outreach to Americans, for example, for disseminating demonstration notices and travel advisories. They strongly opposed the U.S. Embassy's practice of posting content in Arabic on its social media sites (claiming it should be posted exclusively in English) and disseminating U.S. government statements, which they felt triggered unnecessary anti-American commentary. One e-mail sent to the public affairs section stated that although it was unfortunate that Bahrainis were not able to exercise freedom of speech in their own country, Embassy Manama's Facebook page was not the place to allow them to do so.

Social Media: Lessons Learned in Bahrain

The challenges of press outreach in a volatile and rapidly changing environment in Bahrain highlighted the importance of a carefully crafted and well thought out media strategy. One of the major lessons learned is that in order to quickly adapt to a new press climate, a public affairs section must be able to quickly assess how it can most effectively engage with local audience, which tools it can use, and how and at what level engagement can occur. While social media can be a useful in situations like the one in Bahrain, it is nevertheless important to examine how and to what degree the Embassy can and should participate in global and local conversations, taking into account its rules of engagement with online interlocutors and potential blowback from its online engagement.

When planning and executing social media strategies, public diplomacy officers must carefully consider how an Embassy will use social media in crisis situations. Although the Embassy in Manama had a general social media strategy, it had not integrated social media into its crisis management planning. An effective social media strategy should also address questionable material posted on an Embassy's social media sites or postings that are severely critical of U.S. policies. If possible, these conversations should include other sections in the Embassy, particularly with regard to policy discussions on social media sites and possible political fallout.

Another lesson from Bahrain is that active involvement in social media outreach—namely, the generation of original content for various social media sites—requires a full-time staff position. This is even more critical if social media interaction is to take place in a local language instead of in English. Prior to February 2011, Embassy Manama's social media outreach was a collective responsibility of all Public Affairs Section staff, which limited the amount of attention that could be paid by any one staff member.

Additionally, it is important that meaningful metrics be established to evaluate the effectiveness of social media outreach. Counting "likes" on Facebook or "follows" on Twitter does not necessarily ensure that Public Affairs Sections actually know their audiences' perspectives, nor does it necessarily reflect attitudinal changes of local populations. It is also essential to assess whether social media is indeed the most effectual means of outreach. In a small country like Bahrain, for example, one must ask whether social media engagement is more valuable and effective than one-on-one interaction.

Social media is an important public diplomacy tool, and Secretary Clinton has strongly supported its use. However, it is critical that social media engagement be evaluated in relation to the broader policy goals of the Embassy. Policy objectives and public diplomacy activities must be in lockstep. At times it seems that the zeal for public diplomacy outreach—and of late, using social media engagement—can be at odds with achieving policy goals. If public diplomacy practitioners can achieve the careful and strategic integration of policy implementation and social media use, they will be able to excel in communication that bridges the last three *digital* feet.

Notes

1. Government of Bahrain 2010 Census,
   http://www.census2010.gov.bh/results_en.php. Accessed February 11, 2012.
2. Bahrain Independent Commission of Inquiry, *Report of the Bahrain Independent Commission of Inquiry,* 2011, p. 13.
   http://files.bici.org.bh/BICIreportEN.pdf. Accessed February 11, 2012.
3. U.S. Department of State, *Background Note: Bahrain.* (January 13, 2012). http://www.state.gov/r/pa/ei/bgn/26414.htm. Accessed February 11, 2012. See also the Pew Forum on Religion and Public Life, *Mapping the Global Muslim Population: A Report on the Size and Distribution of the World's Muslim Population,* October 2009, p. 10.
   http://www.pewforum.org/newassets/images/reports/Muslimpopulat ion/Muslimpopulation.pdf. Accessed February 11, 2012.
4. A copy of the National Action Charter may be obtained at http://www.pogar.org/publications/other/constitutions/bahrain-charter-01e.pdf.
5. The 2002 constitution established a bicameral legislative branch in which the 40 members of the upper house *(Majlis Al-Shura),* who

are appointed by King Hamad bin Isa Al Khalifa, have oversight over the 40 members of the elected lower house *(Majlis Al-Nuwab)*.

6. Fuad Khuri, *Tribe and State in Bahrain: The Transformation of Social and Political Authority in an Arab State* (Chicago: University of Chicago Press, 1980), p. 5.

7. In the aftermath of the crackdown against Bahraini protesters in mid-March, the Bahraini regime tore down the Pearl Roundabout, reconfigured the streets leading to it, and renamed the juncture as the "GCC Roundabout." The image of the Pearl Roundabout monument continues to provoke tension.

8. Bahrain Independent Commission of Inquiry, *Report of the Bahrain Independent Commission of Inquiry*, 2011, p. 88. Available at http://files.bici.org.bh/BICIreportEN.pdf. Accessed February 11, 2012.

9. The Bahrain Radio and Television Company operates three television channels. The other two include an English language channel and a sports channel.

10. Dubai School of Government, *Arab Social Media Report*, vol. 1, no. 1, January 2011, p. 18. http://www.dsg.fohmics.net/en/Publication/Pdf_En/ASMR_Final_F eb_08Low.pdf. Accessed February 26, 2012.

11. Dubai School of Government, *Arab Social Media Report*, vol. 1, no. 2, May 2011, p. 5. http://www.dsg.fohmics.net/en/Publication/Pdf_En/DSG_Arab_Soci al_Media_Report_No_2.pdf. Accessed February 26, 2012.

12. Ibid, pp. 17 and 19.

13. One notable episode of *Al-Rased* publicly accused the editor-in-chief of the Shi'a opposition newspaper, *Al-Wasat*, of publishing fabricated news stories. The editor-in-chief and two other editors were charged under Bahrain's press law for falsification of news and were also accused of "inciting sectarianism." The editor-in-chief was forced to resign, and *Al-Wasat* was temporarily suspended, making Bahrain's press climate markedly monochromatic for a short time.

14. Reporters Without Borders, *Internet Enemies*, 2011. http://en.rsf.org/surveillance-bahrain,39748.html. Accessed March 1, 2012.

15. Reporters Without Borders, *Press Freedom Index 2011–2012.* http://en.rsf.org/press-freedom-index-2011-2012,1043.html. Accessed March 1, 2012.

16. Michael Slackman, "Security Forces in Bahrain Open Fire on Protesters," *New York Times*, February 18, 2011. http://www.nytimes.com/2011/02/19/world/middleeast/19bahrain.ht ml?pagewanted=all. Accessed March 1, 2012.

17. As a result of the declared State of National Safety, many Bahrainis were being tried in military courts instead of civilian courts.

4

Recapturing the Narrative in Turkey

Elizabeth McKay

As a longstanding NATO ally, a growing and vibrant G20 economy, and a secular and democratic Muslim majority country, Turkey's importance as a strategic partner of the United States is evident. Turkey's increasing role as a regional power has made smart U.S. engagement with the Turkish public all the more critical. In the past decade, addressing the issues of Turkish public opinion toward the United States and Turkish perceptions of the United States have been essential to sustaining and strengthening our partnership.

Negative Turkish public opinion toward U.S. policies had been growing for a number of years, notably since the initiation of hostilities in Iraq in 2003. In part, the Turkish public vehemently opposed the American military action that was taking place on its borders.

Further inflaming public opinion were Turkish perceptions that the United States had failed to adequately support Turkey in confronting domestic terrorist attacks from the PKK. By 2007, a Pew Global Attitudes Poll revealed that as few as 9 percent of the Turkish public had positive views of the United States. Other polls taken during the 2006–2010 period painted a similarly negative picture. Public opinion polling likely reflected one of the valleys of a bilateral relationship that could be characterized by the hills and valleys of any long-term partnership. This particular valley was long and deep, and the erosion in public support for the United States directly threatened our ability to engage on a broad range of foreign policy priorities.

The public affairs environment was one in which Turkish society, itself polarized by domestic challenges, was increasingly vocal about and suspicious of U.S. motives and policies. Feeding on traditional suspicions of the West, epitomized by the United States, self-interested players in Turkey successfully harnessed those suspicions to the detriment of America's image. A dynamic Turkish media also played a significant role in enabling Turkish society's estrangement from the United States.

Strategic re-engagement with the Turks was critical, particularly with its youth. We could not risk the negative polarization of the future generation of Turkish public opinion makers and partners. A key objective for the Mission was recapturing the public narrative about the United States in order to create greater awareness of the positive aspects of U.S. society and culture in general and the U.S.–Turkish relationship in particular. Public diplomacy was the strategic lynchpin of this essential Mission objective.

In 2006, the public affairs officer laid out for the State Department the challenges we faced in reversing the negative trends in public opinion and the need for additional resources to broaden and deepen our contacts with the Turkish people. In response, the Office of the Under Secretary of State for Public Diplomacy and Public Affairs (R) allocated additional, post-specific public diplomacy funding for PD efforts in Turkey, essentially doubling our discretionary program budget. However, due to the legislative authorities governing this account and the separate appropriation to the Education and Cultural Affairs Bureau (ECA), the Mission was not able to utilize post program funds for ECA professional and academic exchanges that we knew to be effective and for which experienced exchange professionals, backed by a longstanding infrastructure, existed. Absent this option, post took on the challenge of establishing a homegrown public diplomacy campaign to re-establish trust and open new avenues of engagement with a Turkish public that was measurably disinclined to engage with us.

Our strategy was to demonstrate to our audiences the increasingly diverse nature of the U.S.–Turkish relationship—one built on a much broader foundation than the security and military alliance that had defined the bilateral relationship for many Turks. Our tactic was to strengthen and expand our people-to-people outreach and to put a greater emphasis on geographic and socioeconomic inclusion that would reach audiences previously underrepresented in USG engagement efforts. Historically, Turkish participation in USG public diplomacy programs was limited to a narrow subset of Turkish society that had the combination of the requisite English language skills and internationally oriented mindset to reach out and fully participate in the program. Our new programs were largely designed to reach beyond these traditional audiences. These efforts came at a time when social media, spreading at a rapid pace, could either negatively or positively affect public opinion. We needed to get out in front of this phenomenon and use it to show America's face.

We recognized that if we addressed the problem from the sole perspective of what we wanted, our efforts would be less successful than if we approached things from the perspective of what our audiences wanted from us. This was an important consideration, and where we deviated from that philosophy, our efforts were less successful. Our campaign had to convey the very positive story we had to tell about the breadth of our relationship, especially as it applied to youth and particularly to the educational, cultural, and commercial sectors. It was a campaign to highlight the "privatization" of the U.S.–Turkish relationship.

With the broad latitude we were given to create field programs, we developed a series of ten pilot projects, many of which were innovative in 2006–2008 but elements of which have now, independently, become mainstays of public diplomacy programs worldwide. The nature of the Foreign Service assignments system is such that four teams of PD professionals played a role in the campaign, from the initial identification of the challenge and the bid for funding in 2006, to the conceptualization and implementation in 2007–2008, and finally the sustainment, expansion, or modification of the key programs from 2009 to the present day. As a team we experimented with approaches that were unconventional and took some risks with the full knowledge that some of our efforts might not succeed. When the funding arrived in late 2007, the PD team on the ground had just eleven months to launch the projects. For the purposes of this case study, I will focus on three of the ten projects.

Youth Innovation and Entrepreneurship

The first project, the Youth Innovation and Entrepreneurship Program, YIEP as it is known today, was one of two flagship programs designed by the PD team. We knew from experience that Turks prized opportunities to advance their education, and exchanges were seen as a prestigious, cost-free vehicle for that opportunity. Our goal in designing YIEP was to promote entrepreneurship and innovative thinking among high school students. Entrepreneurship and innovation require analysis, and we believed that encouraging critical analysis would not only be in the interest of the United States, it would also benefit future generations of Turks and give them important 21st century skills. For the YIEP program, our outreach was expanded to include a heavy focus on regions where students would otherwise have little to no opportunity to participate in a USG program or would have limited direct exposure to Americans and not know America beyond conventional stereotypes. We had a good story to tell about our relationship with Turkey but getting heard required not only a vehicle for delivery of that message, it required a listener willing and able to think through an avalanche of negative information and existing misconceptions.

In the YIEP project, we awarded grants to Junior Achievement and to the Turkish Educational Association to develop and pilot parallel projects in Turkish high schools. The projects trained teachers in seventeen public high schools to coach students on the fundamentals of business education and entrepreneurship. The projects also provided students with hands-on experience through the establishment of their own school-based companies and through the development, financing, marketing, trading, and selling of their companies' innovative products. The grantees added a technological component by providing opportunities for Turkish and American students to trade products and ideas online and through joint venture companies. The high school teams then competed at a regional business fair at which students shared their products and had the opportunity to consult with leading businesspeople and entrepreneurs regarding their ideas.

This project was a winner—the products developed by the students were indeed innovative, clever, and in some cases marketable. Fun, exciting, and educational, this project succeeded at the audience level because it provided an avenue of opportunity for students. It was innovative in that it was created at a time before entrepreneurship was a major emphasis of PD programs. YIEP proved to be a huge success and has been renewed and expanded in recent years. Currently it is operating in 22 provinces at 63 schools throughout Turkey. An online Internet component has been added linking American and Turkish youth. Most recently, it was a core component of the Youth Entrepreneurship Summit that ran concurrently with the Global Entrepreneurship Summit in Istanbul. Teams representing 15 countries in the Middle East and Europe participated in the Summit, many of them with PD support from their local U.S. Embassy. We estimate that over the course of four years, over 5,000 students have participated in YIEP. The Turkish Board of Education has recently signaled that it will formally adapt the YIEP curriculum into its schools as a course elective showing its buy-in to the program.

Youth Filmmakers

The second project was the Youth Filmmakers project. Turkish youth, like youth elsewhere, want to be heard. The filmmakers project gave them an opportunity to convey their views on an international stage on issues they cared about. It gave us a vehicle for promoting linkages, and encouraging critical thinking and freedom of expression.

After an extensive development of the call for proposals, including significant collaboration between the PD teams in Istanbul and Ankara, we awarded a grant to SUNY—the State University of New York (Fredonia)— and a Turkish film company for an 18-month project to teach filmmaking using broad themes of universal appeal among youth: environmental protection, cultural diversity and tolerance, empowering women and girls, economic opportunity, and democracy, among others. The grantee organization, in partnership with the Embassy, selected participants between the ages of 16 and 25. The call for application was targeting any young person interested in filmmaking. Regional and socioeconomic diversity were important elements of the selection criteria. Interviews were conducted by the grantee in each of six cities. Seventy-two students were selected from those 450 candidates who were invited to the interviews. Students with disadvantaged backgrounds and no previous film experience were selected based on their communication skills and enthusiasm. Most of the selected students had never before used a camera.

In each community, three film teams were created and three short films of 5–19 minutes duration were produced. The SUNY team provided the students with approximately 21 days of intensive training in their home cities as well as brief sessions in Ankara and Istanbul, including a session with ECA's American Documentary Showcase directors who were in Turkey on a separate Embassy program. After this intensive training in digital filming and documentary filmmaking, students were asked to create films about important issues for their communities. Eighteen of the 72 students were subsequently selected to participate in a brief internship at SUNY working with American students. At SUNY Fredonia the Turkish students augmented the filmmaking techniques they had learned in Turkey with additional skills in the areas of sound mixing, graphic design, etc. During their two weeks' stay in the United States, they also fine-tuned their films and participated in film festivals. At the end of the project, all 72 Turkish participants and seven SUNY students reunited for three days in Ankara and two days in Konya for discussion, interaction, assessment, and the films' screenings.

Throughout the project, we enjoyed extensive positive media coverage of the project, in part, due to the tremendous interest of the Turkish people in the project and in the Turkish-American heritage of the project coordinator, a professor of film at SUNY. In the final phase of the project, the films were screened in Turkey and in the United States—in Ankara, Fredonia, Istanbul, and Washington, DC, among other cities. This last phase also garnered significant media exposure in Turkey. Films were screened at more than 60 festivals, including the Buffalo International Film Festival, Istanbul Teen International Film Festival, International Youth Media Summit in Belgrade, Akbank Film Festival in Istanbul, First International Film Festival in Bursa, Santa Cruz Film Festival, National Film Festival for Talented Youth in Seattle, If Film Festival in Istanbul, and the Istanbul Short Film Festival. (For further information on the festivals and awards please visit www.filmturkey.net.) The films are still circulating, and once they complete their cycle of screening, will be available online.

Beyond the energy, exposure, and the excitement surrounding this project, the messages conveyed in the films covered a full spectrum of responses. They were inspirational, moving, sad, comic, and hopeful. The best of the films spoke to international audiences with universal messages. The films addressing environmental issues drew the most interest by the international community. We inspired creativity and gave Turkish youth a different lens through which to address current challenges they face. In addition, the long shelf life of the films and their broadcast potential have helped create a young filmmaker program legacy that serves to inspire other potential young filmmakers while simultaneously sparking continued thoughtful discussion in and around the issues the films raised.

The Wiki

The third project, The Wiki, was a social media experiment. In 2007 the median age in Turkey was approximately 22.3 years, a majority of which were urban dwellers. Research revealed that the youth audience, ages 15 to 25, averaged a significant number of online hours each day. How could we reach this very connected audience in a non-obtrusive and credible way? The solution, in our view, was the creation of a platform connecting Turkish and American youth. Once off the ground, our role was to be solely that of facilitator. We funded the creation of a "wiki" through a local youth organization and populated the site with information about our traditional exchange programs, scholarships, and cultural programming as well as promotional and logistical information about some of the new pilot projects. Turkish students could register to participate or compete for the programs and, once selected, could communicate with us and with each other about their programs via our site. Our objective was to make the site a diverse platform for broader communication but the exchanges component— what the audience wanted—was the significant draw. We had high hopes for this new tool but, ultimately, it was less successful than some of the other projects.

We built it, they came, and then—they left. Why? We had provided incentives for young people to visit the site but not enough of a reason for them to stay. It was not organic—it was too artificial a place for communication in an increasingly competitive environment where other spaces were natural conveners of youth. What worked against us was that we built a goal-oriented site maintained by us rather than a true communication platform, maintained by our target audience. Monitored communication was also a deterrent as users felt reluctant to be open about their opinions. Another major challenge was marketing the site to increase its fan base.

Another reason for the lukewarm response to our social media experiment was that we had approached the project as a solution to one of our challenges and not as a solution to the needs of Turkish youth. In short, we were addressing our problem, not the audience's problem. While the project worked in its narrow goal of establishing a social media communication platform for our exchange participants, it failed in the larger goal of becoming an enduring platform for exchange between young Turks and young Americans. Looking back from today's world where social media is an essential tool of communication and mega-sites dominate the Internet, it seems obvious that our project would not have had a sustainable draw. We must remember that five or six years ago, in 2006–2007, the use of social media by governments was in a relative state of infancy and far from the engagement staple it has become today.

Lessons Learned

What were the lessons learned from our overall efforts on these projects?

We learned to approach the design of our programs with the audience's needs in mind—rather than merely our own.

We learned that effective programming must be ongoing and sustainable, and that collaboration with colleagues in the field and at headquarters was key—as was strong partnership with capable implementing partners. These projects were initiated, conceptualized, implemented, and sustained across three, and now four public diplomacy staffs. They never belonged to one public affairs officer, one cultural affairs officer, or one information officer. Rather they were the result of the thoughtful and enthusiastic participation of several PD teams of American officers and the highly talented locally employed staff who were committed to the Mission goals and who embraced the effort to try innovative approaches. The critical buy-in included strong support from the Embassy Front Office, the Department, the European Bureau, and the Office of the Undersecretary for Public Diplomacy. On a daily basis, the EUR Public Diplomacy desk officers in Washington were active participants in the campaign. Public diplomacy desk officers drew the linkage between our programs, Mission Strategic Plan goals and wider department policies, which led to the expansion of other existing programs and strengthened our engagement throughout Turkey. They provided enthusiastic advocacy for the programs, insight into the Department's views of our efforts, program status updates to R and EUR, and served as a sounding board for the post. Our desk officers were essential members of the team without whose direct engagement; these programs might not have received the funding or support needed to carry them beyond the pilot stage.

Another lesson reaffirmed for us was the higher relative value of sustained programs over one-off, stand alone programs that, while often excellent and important in message delivery or for use in limited settings, can lose their impact shortly after completion. As an example, the American storytellers, a pilot project not examined in this paper, provided outstanding speakers who shared important stories about the American experience past and present. By not linking this series to other programs, we perhaps forfeited an opportunity to maximize its impact. That said, we had to make choices on where to put our efforts and limited means. In an ideal world of unlimited human and financial resources, we would have benefited from taking the stand-alone programs, such as the storytellers, further.

Importantly, many of the "gatekeeper" factors found in many of our public diplomacy programs were eliminated for these projects. Neither the Young Filmmakers' program nor the YIEP required English language proficiency. In both cases, the grantee organizations reached out locally, working through local municipal and educational authorities to identify and select program participants (in collaboration with the Mission), administer the programs, and work with the media. The bulk of both of these programs were run in context, within the identified localities where the participants lived. The issues covered were real and contextually very prominent and relevant. Most of the training, production work, and public exhibition of the work was done on a local basis. However, both these programs also included multiple capstone events beyond the localities where the work took place that served to show the end products to a much wider, an often international, audience.

Results

The programs that were a success really helped us to expand our contact base in Turkey. Because of YIEP connections that we made throughout the country, we were able to dovetail ECA-funded exchange programs like Fulbright English Teaching Assistants, the Kennedy-Lugar Youth Exchange and Study, and ACCESS micro-scholarships to give young Turks better access to English language education and give them opportunities for study in the United States—opportunities that were not afforded them before.

How were results measured? We kept the standard post-program surveys as a measurement tool. We also received some unsolicited and graphic accounts of what Turkish youth thought of the United States before and after their participation in our programs. We monitored news coverage of the programs. We also looked at the tenor and content of public commentary, and the opinion polls, which, while improved, continue to seesaw as events beyond our control dictate. However, we understood that polling was a snapshot of sentiment at a given moment in time and not adequate to capture the nuanced and complex nature of collective or even individual feelings towards the United States. We could have bolstered measurements of program effectiveness by doing follow-up surveys with participants (individual and institutional) over a sustained period of time, in order to identify the actual long-term impact.

We also understood that our programs, our long-term investment in people, were important points of entry to the newer generation. The programs played an important part in shoring up the foundation of our relationship with Turkey so that it could better weather the inevitable storms inherent in any long-term relationship.

Five years since the actual launch of these programs, Turkey's position in the world has grown dramatically. True, it has always resided at the crossroads between East and West, geographically; however, today with its foreign policy and economic influence, it stands poised to exert an even greater influence on emerging markets, the new Middle East and Asia. It is therefore of even greater importance that we remain actively engaged in outreach programs that target not only youth but also those that are representative of the "new" Turkey. Influencing them and encouraging positive attitudes about the United States will have a spillover effect to other areas of the relationship.

These programs helped knit live, lasting, and meaningful bonds within the participant communities. The links and impact went far beyond the program participants or the institutions with which they were affiliated. The involvement of media, government officials, artists, business people, educators, and others from the communities where the projects took place made positive impressions that will last for many years to come. The programs not only helped demonstrate how the United States is a good partner and collaborator, but also that the United States is genuinely interested in the people of Turkey. This message came up time and again in interviews with program participants and other community leaders and is often the first thing raised in conversation when the United States is mentioned in these communities. These programs were examples of "people diplomacy" at its best.

5

The Story of "@America"

Michael H. Anderson

Because of 9/11, we began pulling inward. Embassies were fortresses. We don't have the American Corners and Centers that we used to have in abundance that people could walk in and learn about America. So we said we've got to do this differently. Where do people go? So we put an American Center in the biggest mall in Jakarta.

And at first people said, "Oh, my gosh. What does that mean?" Well, it means that we're going to take America's message to where people actually live and work.

—Secretary of State Hillary Clinton, *Time Magazine*,
October 27, 2011

For several decades, public diplomacy officers in Jakarta, Indonesia, and many other U.S. embassies and consulates around the world had a special tool—a cultural center—to use to help build bridges of understanding with diverse local audiences. These publicly accessible, brick-and-mortar structures—usually called "American Centers"—strengthened understanding of U.S. policy, society, and values by providing space for local opinion makers and up-and-coming leaders and students to exchange ideas with Americans and for all to listen and learn from one another.

At the typical American Center, usually centrally located in the heart of a country's major city, visitors could read U.S. books and periodicals, view films and exhibits, hear speakers, enjoy cultural programs, and practice American English. These time-tested, often very lively centers resulted from a diplomatic recognition that the best way to engage audiences and promote understanding was through direct, people-to-people interaction—Edward R. Murrow's critical "last three feet" of effective information and cultural efforts abroad.

These freestanding, high profile facilities were sometimes targets for anti-U.S. demonstrations, but in most settings, cooperation between U.S. Embassy and host-country officials helped ensure that the facilities were protected and remained open to serve the many local end-users who welcomed the programs and services.

By the late 1990s, however, a combination of factors—the end of the Cold War, budget cuts, increased security concerns, the October 1, 1999, consolidation of the USIA into the Department of State, changes in the technology and communication environment, etc.—led to the closure of numerous American spaces, including cultural centers and libraries once open to the public.

The result was hardly a "peace dividend." Many public diplomacy officers were forced to work with both reduced budgets and reduced public programming space, and they had little choice but to retreat behind high Embassy walls. Many American cultural centers shut down, and many public libraries were closed or converted to smaller, less accessible, and more research-focused Information Resource Centers or into American Corners, which were mini-reference libraries hosted by local institutions on non-U.S. government premises.

In the post-9/11 environment especially, security took precedence over all other factors. Not surprisingly, personal interaction and the building of continuity with both traditional elites and younger contacts and the showcasing of the best of America quickly became more difficult.

The quality and quantity of programming and other outreach efforts generally declined as people in droves stayed away from official U.S. premises, which increasingly were perceived as relatively "isolated," "unwelcoming" and "fortress-like."[1] Despite pleas from many contacts and from experienced public diplomacy officers and ambassadors who understood the continued value of centers and the human dimension and relevance of the "last three feet," those who decided budget, space, and security issues felt they had no alternative but to pursue risk management and other policies which sent out a clear signal: the United States could no longer maintain easily accessible places.

Critics of the USIA and its U.S. Information Service (USIS) offices, which had managed press and educational and cultural activities abroad until their merger into the Department of State, argued that such venues were no longer needed and were a waste of money since the Soviet Union had collapsed and the United States was now the world's only superpower.

More recently, after years of debate and numerous reports by one expert panel after another, the "PD space issue" has seen some real movement away from more than a decade of neglect and toward a greater recognition that public diplomacy can make the Department of State more effective. Congress—led by veteran internationalists like Senators Richard Lugar, John Kerry, and several interested Hill staffers—has shown interest in re-examining the PD platform strategy with a goal of re-establishing publicly accessible American Centers. Supporters argued that, in light of the rise of post-9/11 anti-Americanism in much of the world, public diplomacy and good old-fashioned face-to-face communication were needed more than ever to strategically foster mutual understanding and promote peace and stability.

The long overdue reassessment was, in part, a realization that so-called "traditional" public diplomacy practices are still relevant and, in part, a realization that 21st century statecraft needs to make an expanded concept of public diplomacy a core diplomatic mission, with new emphasis on connection technologies and more people-to-people partnerships.

In 2010, the State Department's first Quadrennial Diplomacy and Development Review (QDDR) said, "To do their jobs, American diplomats must have the right tools, adequate resources, and the flexibility to try new approaches." According to the QDDR, the Department is "strengthening and expanding American Centers/Corners: We are identifying the best means of upgrading and maintaining publicly accessible, secure American Centers/Corners and designing models for new American Centers in partnership with the private sector."

Also, the QDDR said that the State Department will "establish a new paradigm for risk management" that will "lead to a comprehensive and responsible construct for managing risk that allows our personnel the flexibility they need to complete mission objectives within a country and to establish new platforms for outreach beyond the Embassy and capital."

Then-Under Secretary for Public Diplomacy and Public Affairs Judith A. McHale, responding to this renewed interest as well as to pressures from the field to reopen the

"PD space" debate, decided to support an exciting public diplomacy pilot project conceived by the U.S. Embassy in Jakarta, capital of the Southeast Asian nation of Indonesia. On December 2, 2010, during a trip to Jakarta, she opened "@America," the world's first high-tech American cultural center, in commercial mall space. Her support of the effort from conception through completion has been crucial.

Recognizing that diplomats need to move beyond the walls of our embassies to speak with people from all backgrounds and walks of life, Under Secretary McHale funded the U.S. Embassy Jakarta-initiated the @America project. Its implementation meant that for the first time in years, Indonesia had a publicly accessible PD space outside the confines of the American Embassy.

The under secretary also established an American Spaces unit in State's Bureau of International Information Programs (IIP) to support the growth of a range of options for PD space outside embassies and to more actively take U.S. public diplomacy into the "marketplace of ideas." More recently, a new deputy assistant secretary-level position—deputy coordinator for regional coordination and American spaces—was established in IIP to create and instill standards on public diplomacy spaces.

Although many of the "traditional" or full-service U.S. cultural centers and libraries have closed or had their public access restricted, the Department today still manages a hodgepodge of public diplomacy spaces evolving in one form or another. One size certainly does not fit all. According to 2011 IIP data, the United States operates 778 separate public diplomacy venues: 177 Information Resource Centers; 37 Centers; 436 American Corners (mini-reference centers off U.S. government premises); and 128 Bi-national Centers (in Central and South America).

Google's Liquid Galaxy, on loan for 2 years, allows visitors to float through Google Earth in a 3D-like environment.

In June 21, 2011, remarks to the Council on Foreign Relations in New York, Under Secretary McHale explained the changed—and changing—PD challenge:

In years past, we were content to wait for the world to come to us. We expected that they would. And when we were the most attractive option, perhaps they did. Not anymore. Today we must contend with an increasingly savvy and motivated set of influencers on a global stage, each armed with a vast array of affordable and adaptable tools to spread their message. Powers such as China, Brazil, and Iran are flexing their economic and political muscle and establishing their own networks of cultural centers and language instruction around the world. We also have to counter lone extremists who pump their ideas into circulation as easily as legitimate actors. These new challenges force us to ask: How do we stand out and respond in such a crowded and complex environment? Our answer is simple: By taking our public diplomacy into the marketplace of ideas.

Indonesia was an ideal venue to revitalize—or, more accurately, to reinvent—the idea of the American Center and to start the first new kind of American Center in years. Its popular public libraries/cultural centers in Jakarta and the two consulate cities of Surabaya in East Java and Medan in Sumatra—operated for years by USIS—had long been closed, and, over the past decade or so, the country had transformed itself from military-run authoritarianism under

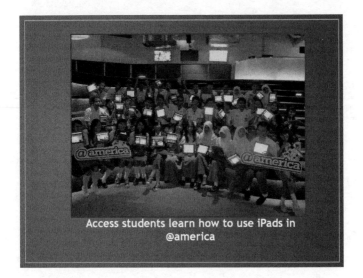

Access students learn how to use iPads in @america

"New Order" President Suharto (1967–98) into a remarkably stable, vibrant democracy under President Susilio Bambang Yudhoyono. From its early post-Dutch colonial days as an independent nation and founding member of the Non-Aligned Movement (NAM) in 1955 under the "Old Order" of President Sukarno (1945–67), Indonesia had progressed into Southeast Asia's largest country and market-based economy and leader of the Association of Southeast Asian Nations.

Not only was the Embassy in Jakarta strongly behind @America, Indonesia itself was ready for more meaningful, post-Cold War interaction with America and an end to lingering historical suspicions. This was clearly demonstrated by the evolving U.S.–Indonesia Comprehensive Partnership signed by Presidents Obama and Yudhoyono in November 2010 and reaffirmed a year later when Obama made his second official visit to Indonesia.

The agreement reflected the Obama Administration's strategic view from the outset that the United States needed to increase substantially its investment in the Asia-Pacific region and specifically in important emerging powers like Indonesia, as well as China and India.

An enduring and dynamic partnership with Indonesia should take on increased importance for the United States as the two countries cooperate to address ongoing global economic problems, political transitions, and other transnational challenges. It was no accident that Secretary of State Clinton's first official overseas trip in early 2009 was to Asia and included a stop in Indonesia, which she has called one of "the most dynamic and significant democratic powers of Asia." According to Secretary Clinton, the United States is:

forging a new partnership with Indonesia, the world's third-largest democracy, the world's most populous Muslim nation, and a member of the G-20. We have resumed joint training of Indonesian Special Forces units and signed a number of agreements on health, educational exchanges, science and technology, and defense.

Another arguably important influence on the improved bilateral relationship was Indonesia's renewed interest in the United States following the election of President Obama, who personally was wildly popular in Indonesia due to the well-publicized fact that young "Barry" Obama had spent four of his formative childhood years there. His American mother, Ann Dunham Soetoro, whose second husband was an Indonesian, conducted University of Hawaii/East–West Center PhD anthropological field research in rural Java and lived and worked in Jakarta while her young son attended local primary school from 1968–1971. According to the president's autobiography, his mother, who went on to become a microfinance program and women's development expert, used to bring him to the library in the U.S. Embassy, where he would learn about America by perusing magazines. On his first presidential trip to Jakarta in November 2010, he recalled the impact Indonesia had had on him: "Because Indonesia is made up of thousands of islands, and hundreds of languages, and people from scores of regions and ethnic groups, my time here helped me appreciate the common humanity of all people."

The two presidents—each of whom had studied in the other's country and knew the other's language—realized the U.S.–Indonesia relationship deserved a more respectful partnership and more strategic attention in the 21st century. Indonesia, after all, was the world's fourth largest nation (population: 240 million); the world's largest Muslim-majority nation (more than 86 percent of Indonesians follow Islam); a moderate, emerging free-market democracy; and—with its recently acquired G-20 membership and its influence in multilateral groups like the East Asia Summit (EAS) and APEC—an increasingly important regional and global player on everything from counterterrorism and regional stability to public health and climate change negotiations.

As President Obama explained during his 2010 Indonesia trip:

> . . . *our two countries have far more in common than most people realize. We are two peoples who broke free from colonial rule. We are both two vast nations that stretch thousands of miles. We are both two societies that find strength in our diversity. And we are two democracies where power resides in the people. And so it's only natural that we should be partners in the world.*

After more than a year of intensive Embassy, multi-agency planning and research, @America opened in late 2010 in an effort to begin a new kind of conversation with Indonesians in support of the evolving official partnership. In the venue, visitors were actively encouraged to "Explore. Experience. Express."

A March 5, 2011, *New York Times* article, headlined "U.S. Updates the Brand It Promotes in Indonesia," said the new facility "represents the United States government's first attempt at creating a full-fledged cultural center since the Sept. 11, 2001, attacks. A high-tech, interactive operation heralded as the digital-age successor to the venerable American Cultural Center, it is also American public diplomacy's latest effort to win over young foreigners, especially in Muslim countries."

Today, @America visitors, as unaffiliated walk-ins or invited guests, are welcomed by friendly, young, English-speaking Indonesian "E-guides" and invited to share their interests and concerns. Inside the 1,751 square foot venue, guests are exposed to U.S. technology, videos and photos, interactive games and a variety of live programs designed to facilitate people-to-people exchange and create communities virtually and in real life. Its multi-purpose area can seat about 250 people on bleachers and can accommodate a variety of programming, including guest speakers, performances, discussions, debates, master classes, exhibitions, video conferences, and classes.

Membership counter where visitors can borrow iPads.

Close cooperation in education is a fundamental part of the U.S.–Indonesia Comprehensive Partnership and of the @America project. Student visitors have access to @America–based educational advisors, who provide free, reliable information on study opportunities on U.S. campuses.

This advising service, which runs 5–9 PM Monday–Friday and 11 AM–9 PM on weekends, is provided in an effort to support a very specific U.S. objective in Indonesia: by 2016, the United States is trying to double both the number of Indonesians studying at American universities (currently flat at only about 7,000 students) and the number of American scholars in Indonesia (currently about 200 students) annually. Given Indonesia's size and importance, both of these figures should be much larger.

According to annual IIE "Open Doors" reports on international educational exchange, the number of Indonesians on U.S. campuses peaked in 1997–1998 at 13,282, and the number of Americans studying in Indonesia has fluctuated wildly and has never exceeded 221. Although the number of Indonesian students in the United States increased steadily in the 1980s and 1990s, it generally declined in the 2000s due to a complex combination of factors, including increased marketing competition from countries like Australia, rising U.S. tuition costs, and the widely held, post-9/11 perception that America did not welcome Muslim students and that U.S. student visas were hard to get.

@America differs from the traditional U.S. cultural center in several significant ways. It is strategically located in a major, central Jakarta mall, Pacific Place, and is open during regular shopping center hours. Although open to the general public, @America is geared to students and young professionals ages 15–30 and is a clear recognition of a generational shift and of the growth in Indonesia of tech-savvy audiences who regularly use Twitter, Facebook, and YouTube.

The venue offers a variety of free public diplomacy programs and activities, but it also embraces cutting-edge technology, including teleconferencing and touch-screen monitors. Visitors may borrow iPads to access a variety of U.S. government and other information (from State

Department, Library of Congress, NASA, MoMA, etc.) and the Internet via high-speed Wi-Fi. They can interact with @America not only by physically visiting the venue in the Pacific Place shopping center but also by accessing a special Web site (http://www.atamerica.or.id), a Facebook page and a Twitter page. @America generally Web streams all of its programs.

The emphasis on social media is particularly important in the Indonesian context because young people make up more than 50 percent of the population; Internet penetration is expanding; the country is one of the world's largest Facebook users; and mobile technologies are booming.

Both Washington and the Embassy in Jakarta realize as never before that if the United States is to communicate effectively with young Indonesians in today's competitive and rapidly changing global communications environment, it needs to engage them in ways they find interesting and relevant and creatively use new and social media. @America therefore, is designed to use both traditional and new tools to address a variety of topics—education, media, politics, sports, music and the arts, the environment, business, etc.—that Indonesians say they are interested in and that are based on mutual respect and mutual interest. Increasingly, for example, Indonesian youth support the transition to democracy and want to learn English, study abroad, and engage with the wider world, including America.

Despite unhappiness with U.S. Middle East and some other policies, Indonesians generally are moderate, curious about the United States and willing to discuss issues in person or online. The Pew Research Center released findings July 13, 2011, which showed that a majority of Indonesians—54 percent—expressed positive views of the United States. The

U.S. Embassy Jakarta Facebook, for example, has more fans than any other single U.S. Embassy Facebook page.

@America also emphasizes public-private partnerships. Google, for example, cooperated by loaning Liquid Galaxy technology so visitors can float through Google Earth in a 3D-like environment and by providing its chief technology advocate, Michael T. Jones, as an @America speaker. Cisco supplied TelePresence, its top-of-the-line videoconferencing technology. Early @America partners on environmental programming, for example, included the Sant Ocean Hall from Smithsonian's Museum of Natural History, the NOAA, The Nature Conservancy, World Wildlife Fund, and Conservation International.

The management of @America is unique. The facility was developed through a holistic approach by the U.S. Embassy in Jakarta, in collaboration with Indonesian and American partners and with strong ambassadorial support plus cooperation from and coordination with Diplomatic Security and the Overseas Building Operations Bureau within the Department of State. The Public Affairs Section has the lead within the Embassy, but other offices, such as USAID, the Foreign Commercial Service, and the Foreign Agriculture Service, contribute ideas, co-sponsor events, and share contacts.

An Indonesian firm with private Americans and Indonesians as staff was contracted to design and manage the venue, and it consults closely with the Embassy. An assistant cultural affairs officer in the Embassy's Public Affairs Section oversees the @America initiative fulltime. An @America advisory board from the wider community of stakeholders and Embassy contacts provides voluntary advice.

Has @America been a success? Has it been a dynamic kind of public diplomacy platform that produces measurable results and improves relations? Has it effectively supported strategic objectives, such as youth and Muslim engagement?

The new Jakarta space has been open for about a year and is still very much a work in progress, and it still remains the only one of its kind. During its first six months of operation, @America attracted almost 44,000 visitors who attended one of more than 270 programs, received information from an on-site educational advisor, or learned about U.S. society through various technology platforms. By July 2011, daily total visitors reached 368 people. Seventy percent were aged 15 to 30. As of July, 2011, @America had 14,266 Web site members; 11,711 Twitter followers; and 3,192 Facebook friends.

By November 2011, well before its first anniversary, @America had welcomed its 100,000th visitor and hosted a wide range of high-impact, low-cost programs intended to pay dividends of friendship for decades. And on the education front, for example, there was also some encouraging public diplomacy news. In fiscal year 2011, student visa applications from Indonesians had increased to their highest figure in 10 years, and 95 percent were approved. Also, two education fairs organized in Indonesia by the U.S. government drew more than 20,000 people and representatives from some 100 U.S. colleges and universities.

All @America programming and content on the iPads, touch screen computers, and monitors are related to one or more of five pillars: All about America; American Education; English Language; Environment, Science and Technology; and Innovation and Entrepreneurship.

A good example of a cool, successful @America program with a policy message was an August 2011 event tied to the end of Ramadan, the Islamic fasting month. @America hosted a well-received performance by Native Deen, an American Islamic hip-hop group whose State Department-sponsored visit showcased not only American music but also cultural diversity and religious tolerance. Other creative programs have featured topics as diverse as women entrepreneurship, environmentally sustainable economic growth, climate change, saving the Indonesian orangutans, technology, American literature, cooking, English teaching, development assistance, American pop culture through music and dance, and the observance of Halloween.

The U.S. ambassador and deputy chief of mission in Jakarta often speak at or attend @America events, and a steady stream of officials from Washington and Indonesia has visited the facility and participated in various programs. For example, in late July 2011, IIP Coordinator Dawn L. McCall visited Jakarta to inaugurate a series of focus groups. According to the Department, these sessions were to "gauge the success of @America programs and better understand people's experiences with this new and dynamic American space."

Also, IIP arranged for a Smithsonian exhibits specialist to give @America feedback and advice. IIP's Audience Research Unit has done extensive formal evaluations of @America. Focus groups are positive about programs but desire more quantity and depth of content to be made available in general.

As anticipated, @America managers have had to work hard to promote the facility and have not depended solely on casual, walk-in mall visitors or traditional elite audiences. Sixty-five percent of visitors have been event visitors and 35 percent have been walk-ins. Not surprisingly, much of the most effective programming has happened when specific academic, professional, or cultural or media audiences were invited to specific events.

Security arrangements—an absolute priority for the new facility since day one—have been responsible and adequate, but they have been off-putting to some attendees.

@America needs fine-tuning; sustained funding; a steady supply of relevant, high quality, and timely content; intra-Department coordination; and continued careful monitoring and evaluation and appropriate security. But it is clearly on track as a lab for the Department to try new public diplomacy approaches and as an evolving model for a new generation of American cultural centers and outreach that public diplomacy practitioners and foreign audiences have long awaited.

Indonesian and international media coverage of @America has generally been extensive and positive, and, in bilateral terms, there is no question that @America has actively engaged new audiences and helped advance and highlight the broadening and deepening U.S.–Indonesia relationship, which the Obama Administration feels is one of the most consequential for both countries in the 21st century.

When @America opened in late 2010, then-Under Secretary McHale said she hoped it would be "the first of a new generation of American cultural centers." According to IIP, @America is still considered a pilot project, although other embassy posts are considering aspects of it such as the mall location and the contractor staff. Dhaka, for example, is planning to use contractor staff at a new center it hopes to open, and Riga is looking at opening a small location with a local partner.

In today's challenging era of extremely tight budget constraints, it very much remains to be seen whether the

Jakarta facility—which cost about $5 million to set up and has annual operation costs of about $3 million—will be a one-off experiment or a real model for a different kind of American public space over the long term.

As the Department of State wrestles with scarce resources and coordination problems and continues to test ways to make public diplomacy more effective, public diplomacy advocates generally and supporters of closer U.S.–Indonesia ties specifically hope @America succeeds as a new and attractive kind of American space abroad.

The unique project-in-a-mall has certainly caught the attention of Washington policymakers, including Secretary of State Hillary Clinton. During a July 24, 2011, visit to Indonesia, noting that the project was "something that former Under Secretary Judith McHale was so enthusiastic about, she must have reported to me about it 100 times," the secretary explained, "We closed down American centers all over the world for security reasons, and made it also difficult for people to come to the Embassy or some other location. So now we are going to where people are."

Meanwhile, the Government of Indonesia has said it plans to begin opening its own cultural centers, including one in the United States, and the idea of youth programming and outreach via shopping malls seems to be spreading. On August 16, 2011, Muhtar Kent, Chairman and CEO of Coca-Cola, visited Indonesia and launched his company's Learning Lounge in partnership with an Indonesian nongovernmental organization in Plaza Semanggi, another central Jakarta mall. The venue is designed to provide "a modern welcoming space" for youth to gather for positive learning activities. Learning Lounge, which has books and IT facilities to facilitate learning about the environment and other issues, is open daily during mall hours. Admission is free. On paper at least, the venue sounds a bit like an @CocaCola center.

Notes

1. According to a February 13, 2009, Senate Foreign Relations Committee report, of the 177 "Information Resource Centers" in existence in 2009, 11 percent did not permit public access, and 49 percent operated by appointment only. Data showed centers located outside U.S. Embassy compounds attracted "significantly more" visitors than facilities located inside compounds.

6

The Brazil Youth Ambassador Model

Jean Manes

For many embassies around the world, one of the biggest challenges is how to engage audiences given the level of staffing and monetary resources. The U.S. Embassy in Brazil was no exception. Brazil is a country with approximately 206 million people in 26 states plus the Federal District. The U.S. presence in Brazil consists of the Embassy in Brasilia and three consulates located in Sao Paulo, Rio de Janeiro, and Recife.

This case study highlights the Youth Ambassador Program in Brazil, an exchange program now in its tenth year and recognized as a State Department best practice. In my 20 years in the Foreign Service, it is the best example I have seen that puts the whole package together: exchanges, media, private-sector partnership, alumni outreach, educational advising, Binational Centers that teach English, and local government involvement. It is the combination of these elements that make the Youth Ambassador Program a centerpiece of the U.S.–Brazil relationship.

This case study will explore some essential partnerships that can further the potential of a traditional exchange program by converting it into a centerpiece of U.S. engagement in a country by leveraging various assets and multiplying the engagement well beyond the limited number of participants in an exchange program.

The program today is not how it first started 10 years ago, but it has grown and the impact has increased over the years as feedback from participants was considered and new elements incorporated. It is the goal of this case study to examine these elements to allow others to implement these lessons learned over the past 10 years into initial concept plans for public diplomacy programming while modeling the potential of a 35-person exchange program for countrywide results.

What is it?

The Youth Ambassador Program in Brazil, created in 2002, is a three-week leadership program for young people from the public school system ages 15–17. It is important to highlight that focusing this program on the public school system by de facto targets the underserved populations in Brazil. For the majority of families, the first economic decision is to send their children to private school, which enhances their ability to get into the quality public education system at the university level. While it is now a true "exchange" with participants from both the United States and Brazil, the case study will focus on the Brazilian participants to the United States as that is the most significant portion of the public diplomacy programming. During the three-week program, participants engage in a Washington component where they meet with government officials, visit schools, and participate in social projects. They also strengthen their leadership skills through workshops and lectures. The second component of the experience involves traveling to host states, where they stay with host families, attend classes at local high schools, and participate in volunteer activities. To date, the program has directly benefited over 250 Brazilian young people and has indirectly impacted thousands. In 2012, more than 7,500 public school students applied for 45 slots (the program normally consists of 35 participants annually, but an extra 10 were added as part of the 10-year anniversary commemoration).

The experience of being a youth ambassador gives these outstanding students the opportunity to expand their horizons while strengthening the ties of friendship, respect, and collaboration between Brazil and the United States. The initial goal of the Youth Ambassador Program in Brazil was to target young, future leaders of the communities in Brazil who would, in turn, build a network of youth across Brazil interested in discussing issues of mutual concern.

From the initial vantage point, this looks like a regular exchange program, our public diplomacy bread and butter which has been the foundation of our engagement with other countries for decades. In my opinion, this is why this case study can serve as a model for leveraging partnerships and expanding impact. With almost every public diplomacy section around the world engaged in exchange programs, the ability to transform these exchanges into a centerpiece for the U.S. engagement in that country is definitely possible.

The following describes the essential components that encompass the Youth Ambassador Program in Brazil and elements that should be considered by a public diplomacy practitioner in the conceptualization and implementation of an exchange program.

Key Elements

1. Clear Vision and Leadership

2. Centerpiece of U.S. Engagement
3. Partnerships
4. Recruitment and Selection for the Program
5. Incorporation of Social Media
6. Follow-up
7. Challenges/Lessons Learned

Clear Vision and Leadership

At the foundation of this exchange program is a clear vision and leadership. Although this is not unique to public diplomacy, it is essential to ensure that this is a Mission-wide program and not limited to the Public Affairs Section of the Embassy. The Youth Ambassador Program began with the vision of the former U.S. Ambassador to Brazil, Donna Hrinak, and continues today with the leadership of Ambassador Thomas Shannon. This top level leadership is what facilitates the partnerships that are necessary with the local government, the private sector, and the media. The ambassador is routinely involved in all phases of the program participating in the high profile launch of the program each year and meetings with Youth Ambassador participants and alumni on a regular basis during travel throughout the country.

Centerpiece of U.S. Engagement

In order for the exchange program to be a centerpiece for engagement in a given country, it should incorporate certain core elements and values that embody the U.S.–host country relationship and outreach efforts. For the Brazil model, this includes the following:

- The importance of the public school system in a successful society
- Community service and volunteerism as integral components of society
- The belief that everyone deserves an opportunity regardless of socioeconomic standing

- Young people are the key to the future of any society
- Hard work, integrity, and perseverance pay off
- Engagement of young people with those from other countries is essential to the competitiveness of a society and global understanding
- Once given an opportunity, giving back and mentoring others is expected

As a centerpiece of the U.S. engagement with Brazil, the Mission—not just the Public Affairs Section—recognizes that this program embodies the relationship and that the ambassador places a strong emphasis on it as well. This is important given that so many exchange programs fly under the radar of the rest of the Mission in which they can have a positive, but limited impact.

Partnerships

The U.S. government cannot be a unilateral player in a program that serves as a centerpiece for engagement. Partnerships are essential and add to the multiplier impact as well as serve as a catalyst for other engagement. Developing partnerships is time consuming, but it is a solid investment.

For the Brazil program, partnerships have evolved over the last 10 years and now include the Brazilian government (at the state and local level), private sector, public school system and the media. Since this is the heart of what takes this exchange program to a new level, we'll explore specific areas of partnerships.

The U.S. Embassy

The U.S. Embassy serves as the overall lead for all components of the exchange program, harnessing the players and distinct components. This begins with the U.S. grantee organization that provides the support structure for the program. The grantee organization receives a grant from the State Department to provide logistics and program support for the U.S. portion of the program. Although the Embassy does not subcontract out the strategic thinking or follow-up of the program, it provides the logistical coordination. The Embassy remains very involved in the process, providing input to the U.S. schedule to ensure that it is consistent with the overall objectives of the program. The Embassy must serve as the overall lead for the program if the other components, including the partnerships and follow-up, are to be effective. One primary objective is for the Youth Ambassador participants and alumni to feel a connection with the Embassy. In order for that to happen, the Embassy must be directly involved and willing to build relationships with the participants. This involves a substantial amount of time commitment of local staff in the Public Affairs Section and should be assessed during the initial planning discussion to decide whether the Embassy wants to assume this leadership and responsibility. For the Brazil program, the primary local staff person engaged in the project is known as "Mom Marcia" to the participants and alumni of the program. This exemplifies the level of affection that the participants have for her as a representative of the Mission and represents the type of lasting bond that direct Embassy involvement can create.

Local Government Partnership

For the Brazil model, local government partnership is a central focus as Brazil has 26 states. One primary objective is for the exchange program to have countrywide impact. The only way to do that is to ensure that the participants are recruited from across the country. How do you recruit across the country if the United States has only a direct presence in 4 of 26 states (plus the Federal District)? Partner with local government or institutions with a broad presence.

The Embassy partners with the National Council of State Secretaries of Education in Brazil. The State Secretaries have responsibility for the public school system within their state. They serve as the primary partner and first point of entry for candidates for the program. In addition, the Embassy has a long relationship with the National Council of State Secretaries as a central sponsor of their "Teacher of the Year" program. This partnership builds on these efforts. The State Secretaries and Teachers in the school system view the Youth Ambassador Program as a positive opportunity for their public school students and they understand that it is a well-controlled and fair selection process. By partnering, the State Secretaries provide the important link which enables the program to have countrywide reach. Furthermore, the Embassy makes a specific effort to select at least one participant from each state. The selection of a student from a specific school becomes a badge of honor for them and encourages further recruitment. With 10 years' worth of experience with the program, the best recruiters are the alumni of the program who actively engage with potential new students. We will discuss that in more detail in the social media section.

Brazilian Ministry of Education

There is no substitute for the high level government-to-government cooperation on a program that embodies the bilateral relationship. Education is a strategic pillar in the U.S.–Brazil partnership. While the support is not detailed, as most of the day-to-day negotiations regarding the exchange are at the State level, there is an overarching agreement between the two governments that this exchange is important and valuable. This support facilitates senior-level meetings for the participants of the program and signals the prestige of the exchange.

Private Sector

Both U.S. and Brazilian companies support this program. In the beginning, these negotiations started with the American Chamber of Commerce in Brazil. This provided a valuable group of businesses the opportunity to discuss potential partnership. The Embassy focused on shared interests. Most U.S. companies in Brazil are constantly looking for talented young people and since their recruiting process is thorough and well respected, companies benefit from having access to a talented pool of potential employees. More specifically, the Youth Ambassador Program provides young people with leadership training, an overseas experience, and English—all positive qualities and skills in demand. While a number of companies provide monetary support, the most valuable support is the potential internships and job opportunities for participants in the program. One partner even provides additional online computer training for all Youth Ambassador alumni. Again, this is centered on the focus of shared interests. Instead of approaching the U.S. companies solely for the purpose of funding, the Embassy focuses on areas of true partnership in which they could provide potential applicants for their business needs as well as support their overall corporate responsibility objectives. Building our business partners into marketing opportunities as well as personally engaging with participants in these programs is incredibly important.

Academic Partners

In the Western Hemisphere, public diplomacy has a unique advantage with the existence of Binational Centers. Binational Centers are private, fully independent institutions dedicated to promoting U.S. culture, including the study of English, and the culture of the host country. Their primary support comes from student fees for English classes. Although BNCs do not receive annual base financial support from the U.S. government, they serve as valuable partners for programs and frequently receive funding to implement specific projects in the interest of advancing U.S. foreign policy objectives. These institutions provide quality English teaching and cultural experiences for students across the Hemisphere. In Brazil, we have a network of 38 Binational Centers that teach over 70,000 students a year. The Centers serve as a central partner in both the recruitment phase and the follow-up after the program. During the recruitment phase they advertise for the program, test the level of English of applicants, as well as participate in the home visits of the final candidates. Following the selection and participation in the program, many of the Binational Centers provide free scholarships to Youth Ambassador alumni for them to continue to study and improve their English. Although the majority of Youth Ambassador participants have had limited formal English study, most have learned English on their own through radio, television and the internet- demonstrating their initiative and dedication.

In addition to Binational Centers, academic partners encompass various academies in the U.S. that provide short-term English study as well as other leadership institutes. The State Department has EducationUSA advisors worldwide who provide accurate information to foreign students who are interested in studying in the United States. The student advisors in Brazil have worked over a number of years to develop partnerships with these U.S. institutions and provide scholarships for a select number of Youth Ambassador participants following the program. The scholarships focus on raising their overall English ability. This is a core component, along with the Binational Center scholarships, which provides a ladder for the Youth Ambassador alumni to participate in other U.S. government opportunities. Some of these opportunities include the

Fulbright Undergraduate and Graduate program, summer institutes, and the general possibility of studying in the United States. All require a certain level of English capability.

Media

The media throughout Brazil serve as the platform to publicize the program and demonstrate the impact. The most significant partnership is with Globo (the largest media outlet in Brazil and fourth largest in the world). They have elevated the program to a new level and have demonstrated their commitment to education and youth in Brazil. In recent years, the Embassy has partnered with Globo to send a television crew to the U.S. with the participants. The crew captured the various elements of the program including the meeting with government officials and the homestay experience with U.S. families in various states. In 2010, the crew captured the excitement of the Youth Ambassador participants' meeting with First Lady Michelle Obama in the White House. The First Lady spent more than 30 minutes with the group in an engaging discussion of issues of concern. She also made it a point to meet with Youth Ambassador alumni during the March 2011 visit of the president and first lady to Brazil. In 2010, Globo produced a 50-minute special on the Youth Ambassador Program that aired on the most popular program—*Caldeirao do Huck*. It is fair to say that the exposure on that program is equivalent to what we know as the "Oprah Effect." The program more than quadrupled the following year in the number of applicants to 4,500 and almost doubled again this year to 7,500.

However, media engagement is not simply limited to national television. The program has evolved to encompass a comprehensive media strategy—television, print, and social media. Particular attention will be given to social media later in the case study as it is one of the newer tools of public diplomacy and has been incorporated into every facet of this program.

Recruitment and Selection for the Program

Every facet of the program hinges on the selection process; do we get the right individuals? Hence, the Embassy is directly involved to ensure that the process is fair and incorporates the core values highlighted earlier. Using the network provided by the National Council of State Secretaries of Education, the program is advertised throughout the entire public school network of Brazil. Candidates are selected based on the following criteria:

- Academic excellence
- Proven leadership
- Social responsibility; mandatory requirement of at least one year in a community service project.
- English language ability. This is the most flexible criterion, as the vast majority of applicants have not had the luxury of private English instruction. Moderate English, focusing on the ability to communicate is required.
- Member of an underserved population. The program is specifically designed with the public school system. As a result, most applicants have limited financial opportunities to participate in an exchange program.

Applicants go through a multi-phase recruitment process. Following the explosion of applicants after the television program on Globo TV, the initial application phase moved online. About 150 top applicants move to the final phase and submit an essay that is evaluated as part of the entire application packet reviewed by senior American officials and local staff. Candidates are discussed and consensus reached on the 35 candidates. The 100 that are not selected participate in a special English Immersion program in

Brazil, which consists of a weeklong immersion focusing on U.S. history, geography, society, culture, cooking, and sports. The English camp is run in five different regions of Brazil, utilizing the network of Binational Centers and increasing the impact of the program.

Once selected, the Embassy organizes the high profile announcement. One of the business partners hosts the event that is led by the U.S. ambassador, senior Brazilian government officials, and the private sector partners. In the last few years, the announcement has been carried live on Internet radio as well as video streaming, which have penetration across the country. Participants have often shared stories of their entire family sitting around the radio or watching via computer at their school waiting for the announcement. It is fair to say that the selection of a participant directly impacts the entire family and has a positive impact in their community. Immediately following the announcement, the Embassy works with local media across Brazil to provide contact information for the new participants. Alumni from the program are immediately connected via social media to the new participants in their respective state. They serve as direct mentors as the new participants prepare for the experience. This serves as a central component given that these mentors can directly relate to the overwhelming feelings that participants encounter following the announcement as well as to help them connect with others when they return from the United States.

Local media interview the candidates. After selection into the program, on average each participant gives between 10–15 media interviews (radio, TV, or print) before and following their trip to the United States. This is crucial as these are markets that the U.S. Embassy would rarely reach. The Embassy provides each participant with basic information about the program, including the goals, selection process, details about the U.S. experience, and information on the program sponsors. Many local mayors contact the selectees and host events for them. All media engagement is tracked by the Embassy and shared with key partners.

Incorporation of Social Media

The incorporation of social media into every facet of the program leverages partnerships and amplifies the impact. As mentioned, the use of social media begins at the outset. The program is advertised on all of the Embassy platforms: Web site, Facebook, and Twitter, as well as those of partner institutions. In addition, the Youth Ambassador Program has an alumni network with their own Facebook site.

Since 2010, when the 50-minute special aired on Globo Television, the application process became available online. The Embassy knew that the interest in the program would skyrocket following the airdate. As a result, a team developed the online process with the initial encounter on Facebook. As part of the process, an interested applicant must "friend" the Embassy in order to submit an application for the program. This provides an immediate network of young people that the Embassy can reach out to for other engagement opportunities. One year, the Embassy created a video component that involved the applicants submitting a 3–5 minute video describing their community service project and its importance and impact. The participant who received the most "likes" on their video was selected as part of the program. This allowed the Embassy to highlight the importance of the community service element of the program while encouraging volunteerism.

There are other social media elements, including the five simultaneous Web chats, which followed the airing of the

50-minute special. Globo Television publicized the Embassy Web site at the end of the program to encourage those interested in more information, to go to the site and chat live with coordinators of the program. Over 40,000 people participated in the Web chats in a two-hour period. A combination of Embassy staff and Youth Ambassador alumni monitored the chats providing interested participants with information. In advance, the Embassy circulated basic Q&A information to the staff and alumni to help moderate the chat and provide consistent information. As a result of the sheer volume of interest, the Embassy Web site crashed over the weekend and a new server was installed.

In preparation for the airing of the program and the flocking to the Web site, careful attention was given to ensuring sufficient materials were on the site to provide accurate information regarding the program.

Prior to their travel to the United States, new participants are in constant contact with their mentors via social media. The mentors advise on just about everything. From sharing experiences of what it is like to live with a host family to suggesting what they should pack, the new participants had an opportunity to get the information they needed. Encouraging alumni to take a direct leadership role in mentoring others is a fundamental component and helps build a stronger network of youth across Brazil. Days before their departure, participants gather in a central location of the country and engage in leadership discussion as well as immersion into U.S. culture and society. A social media plan is a core part of these sessions as well as for travel to the United States. There is a regular schedule of Facebook and Twitter engagement that builds on the excitement, as the participants get ready to depart for the United States. Families and friends follow these posts to keep up with the trip of the youth ambassadors. Furthermore, participants are also provided with media instruction so that they can use these tools effectively. In order to disseminate current information regarding their time in the United States, a schedule is developed requiring participants to blog and post pictures about their experiences. This spreads the workload and provides insight from the young people firsthand rather than the Embassy staff.

Embassy personnel and the grantee staff accompany the group to the United States. This ensures that the participants build a personal relationship with the Embassy and that the schedule and meetings directly support Embassy objectives. In addition, the Embassy staff, closely coordinated with the Foreign Press Center at the State Department, provides assistance to traveling media, ensuring that they have the necessary access.

For the last couple of years, Globo Television has selected four participants from the group to serve as their correspondents. The television crew follows these four individuals throughout the trip, while capturing footage of their homestay experience. On the virtual side, the Globo Web site features short biographies and photos of all participants in which the participants blog and post additional material.

Follow-up, Follow-up, Follow-up

There is no more critical component than what happens after the exchange. The Embassy emphasizes to new participants that selection into the program is just the first step. "Once you are a youth ambassador you are always a youth ambassador." At present, there are over 250 alumni of the program in which they remain connected in an official Youth Ambassador alumni network, created by alumni. The Embassy supports alumni efforts through small grants for specific initiatives that focus on areas such as leadership and community service.

The student-advising element of the State Department, EducationUSA, remains as a constant resource to participants as they develop their academic goals. For those interested in studying in the United States, EducationUSA works with them on applications and can secure funding for initial tests and other requirements. Our partner institutions also provide scholarships for short-term courses and many Youth Ambassador alumni have received full undergraduate scholarships to prestigious U.S. universities. For those who want to study in Brazil, the Embassy provides letters of recommendations as well as other guidance.

Beyond the academic guidance, the Embassy facilitates internships and job opportunities through the private sector business partners. This is a dynamic area with an opportunity for growth as U.S. companies expand their presence in Brazil and are in search of talented young people.

Personal follow-up—whether academic advising or internship/job placement—is time consuming. It involves harnessing multiple facets of the Public Affairs Section to remain engaged and committed as part of a comprehensive plan. However, it is doable and worth the investment if the Mission determines that this exchange program is going to represent the centerpiece of the partnership between two countries.

Challenges and Lessons Learned

The Embassy continues to learn and to enhance the program every year. Both participant and partner feedback are core components of the formal process as the information is incorporated into the program design for implementation the following year. Nonetheless, there are a couple of big challenges. The first one is the decision to make this exchange program a centerpiece of engagement. Since the Public Affairs Section at an Embassy has limited staff, running this program requires commitment of resources and personnel. In an effort to focus the necessary attention to develop the partnerships required to implement this program, it may be necessary to weed out or say no to programs that are a lower priority.

The second major challenge regards the target group of this program. Because this program targets public school students ages 15–17, the majority of the participants come from low-income families and face many challenges. Although these students are extraordinary kids with unlimited potential, they are kids. As a result, the Embassy has a much higher level of responsibility in this program versus that of a professional exchange program which targets 25–35 year-old adults. The participants in this program are kids from underserved populations, which makes follow-up all the more important. For example, it is the first international trip for the overwhelming majority of the candidates, and many have never left their hometown. In particular, given the popularity of the program, which is known to make these participants mini-celebrities in their hometown, additional responsibility, sufficient leadership, and follow-up are necessary to ensure that participants are able to handle the effects and impact of the program. To send them on this type of program which creates certain expectations and then not follow-up would be irresponsible. Overall, partnerships with businesses for internships, English scholarships at Binational Centers, small grants for alumni projects, and other initiatives are all designed to continue to engage these young people as they move into adulthood.

Putting it All Together

1. Location of U.S. Embassy and Consulates (Chart 1)
2. Recruitment—select at least one participant from each state (Chart 2)
3. Facebook Friends and Media Interviews—Candidates must friend the Embassy in order to submit their application. On average, each participant has between 400–600 Facebook friends. Once selected, their friends follow their experience through the regular posting of photos and comments. On average each participant gives between 10–15 local media interviews (Chart 3)
4. Partnership with National Media—the Embassy partners with Globo Television—the largest outlet in Brazil and fourth largest in the world. In 2010, the television program "Caldeirao do Huck" produced a 50-minute special on the program. (Chart 4)

Chart 1. Location of U.S. Embassy and 3 Consulates

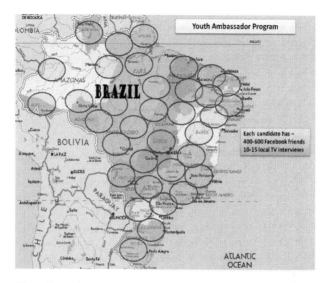

Chart 2. Each participant has 400–600 Facebook friends and engages in 10–15 interviews

Chart 3. Selection of 35 candidates with at least one per state

Chart 4. Partnership with Globo and 50-minute special broadcast across Brazil

Conclusion

An embassy can empower a traditional bread and butter exchange program to serve as a centerpiece for the bilateral relationship between the United States and a host country. The key for this success is to develop a comprehensive strategic plan that begins with the leadership of the Mission and builds partnerships that enhance the impact. Even in a country the size of Brazil, a 35-person exchange program can provide countrywide impact with careful thought and planning given to the recruitment process. Last but not least, the critical components of follow-up and linkage with other embassy assets, such as student advising and alumni engagement, help ensure that the program leverages the impact. This is what Public Diplomacy officers do each and every day around the world on behalf of the American people.

7

U.S. Embassy Baghdad Social Media Outreach

Aaron D. Snipe

Background

With the responsible drawdown of U.S. forces in Iraq to fewer than 50,000 in August 2010 and the shift in the U.S. military's mission from combat to "advise, train, and assist," the relationship between Iraq and the United States underwent a significant transition from one dominated by military and security-related issues to a broader focus on strategic partnership based on shared interests. In his Oval Office address on August 30, 2010, President Obama declared that while our relationship with Iraq is changing, the U.S. commitment to the people of Iraq endures. Fulfilling this promise, President Obama ordered a withdrawal of all U.S. troops by December 31, 2011, thereby paving the way for a more normalized civilian-to-civilian relationship between the governments and peoples of the United States and Iraq. Through the civilian-led efforts of the United States Embassy in Baghdad, the United States continues to work with the Iraqi government and people to implement the Strategic Framework Agreement.[1] While the State Department has maintained a strong civilian presence in Iraq since 2003, U.S. military engagement with the government and people of Iraq has dominated the U.S. government's overall messaging posture. The drawdown (and, eventual departure) of U.S. troops from Iraq presented the U.S. Embassy and its public diplomacy practitioners a window of opportunity to engage the Iraqi population.

The mission of American public diplomacy is to support the achievement of U.S. foreign policy goals and objectives, advance national interests, and enhance national security by informing and influencing foreign publics and by expanding and strengthening the relationship between the people and government of the United States and citizens of the rest of the world.[2]

Security considerations in countries like Iraq and Afghanistan present unique challenges for the practice of public diplomacy in the 21st century. War, the threat of terrorism, and heightened security measures often stand as impediments to public outreach by Foreign Service professionals. Yet, these impediments are not impenetrable. The toolbox of America's public diplomacy professionals has expanded beyond the traditional American Corners and poster shows, and now includes Facebook, YouTube, and Twitter. From Baghdad to Basrah, Kabul to Kandahar, social media has given public diplomacy practitioners a direct line of communication into the offices, coffee shops, and homes of millions people. Through the use of social media, the men and women of the Foreign Service entrusted to carrying American ideas (and ideals) can now engage, inform, influence, and listen to the local population, giving the United States its best chance to bridge what Edward R. Murrow described as "the last three feet."

Social Media in Iraq and the Changing Landscape of Diplomatic Engagement

The momentous events in the Middle East and North Africa in 2011 that are popularly referred to as "the Arab Spring" clearly demonstrated that Facebook, YouTube, Twitter, and other social media platforms had become essential tools in the exchange of ideas among youth across the region. Though far behind countries like Egypt in developing a social media landscape, Iraq is no exception to this recent trend, with social media becoming increasingly popular among Iraqis yearning to connect and communicate. A recent finding on social media by the Dubai School of Government reports that while Internet penetration is still relatively low in Iraq (less than 2 percent), roughly 400,000 Iraqis currently use Facebook.[3]

In order for the U.S. Embassy in Baghdad to communicate effectively with Iraqi youth and keep pace with these fast-moving trends, public diplomacy practitioners on the ground must continue using traditional public diplomacy tradecraft, while also seizing opportunities for engagement provided by social media.

In the summer of 2010, U.S. Embassy Baghdad Public Affairs Section (Baghdad PAS) embarked on a more aggressive campaign to engage the Iraqi public using social media. Challenging long-held assumptions that Internet penetration in Iraq remained too low for useful social media engagement, Baghdad PAS began in earnest to use Facebook and YouTube to accomplish the following objectives:

1. Communicate messages of enduring civilian commitment to the people of Iraq under the U.S.–Iraq Strategic Framework Agreement using Arabic-speaking Foreign Service officers;

2. Participate in an open exchange of ideas with the Iraqi people, targeting youth, women, State Department-exchange program alumni, and Iraqi communities outside of Iraq;
3. Provide a space for an online community of both English- and Arabic-speakers to discuss issues of mutual benefit and interest to the United States and Iraq.

Methodology: Revamping Facebook

Embassy Baghdad launched its Facebook page in January 2010. Baghdad PAS advertised the page in the local Iraqi press to publicize the launch, generating an initial spike in interest. The *Huffington Post* news Web site also ran a short piece on their technology page entitled "U.S. Embassy in Baghdad Hunts for Facebook Friends."[4] Despite positive initial press reporting, the page languished shortly after the launch, with active users plummeting from more than 4,000 in February 2010 to slightly more than 1,000 in June 2010.[5]

A variety of factors contributed to the decline in participation. Chief among them was the absence of a clearly defined social media engagement strategy. Before the summer of 2010, Baghdad PAS had yet to dedicate the necessary personnel and resources to social media initiatives. Additionally, without a social media strategy, the Embassy had not yet clearly defined their audience, nor had they establish social media messaging priorities.

Embassy Baghdad's initial Facebook foray met a number of additional obstacles:

English vs. Arabic: In the initial six months of Embassy Baghdad's Facebook page, information was posted almost exclusively in English, limiting the audience to a tiny number of Iraqi elites, Americans currently or formerly serving in Iraq, and their families and friends back in the United States.

Limiting Content Policy: Baghdad PAS enacted a policy that required all posted material to be USG-generated content, greatly limiting options and interest. Rather than fostering organic dialogues about current events and social issues, the Embassy's Facebook page was severely limited to discussions of (often stilted) official content.

Facebook-by-Committee: A cautious stance toward Facebook led the PAS to create a Facebook Committee that required committee clearance for every item, 24 hours before posting. This blunted Facebook's greatest strength—its timeliness—and resulted in posts that were so anodyne that only a handful of users would comment. The bureaucracy created a situation where weeks passed without activity, resulting in a moribund Facebook page with dwindling engagement.

In June 2010, a new assistant information officer inherited responsibility for the Facebook page. Under the guidance and direction of Baghdad PAS's new leadership, this officer received social media training from the State Department's Bureau of International Information Programs (IIP), daily guidance from the Embassy's deputy public affairs officer and information officer, and quickly addressed the limitations of the old structure.

Steps taken to reinvigorate social media engagement included the following:

Broadened Content: While IIP-generated content remained an important part of Embassy Baghdad's Facebook content, postings were broadened to include non-USG generated content; specifically, Iraq-related content in furtherance of the Mission's objectives of interest primarily to Iraqis. Baghdad PAS launched a number of new initiatives to increase and engage the Iraqi fan-base. Rather than posting passive news stories with no follow-up, Baghdad PAS began piloting discussions on Facebook. A new initiative, entitled "Question of the Day," gave PAS an opportunity to post a current events question in Arabic, encouraging the readership to engage in daily and timely discussions. Questions range from "What do you think about the law banning the hijab in France?" to "What is your favorite kebab shop?" to "What are your thoughts on the proposed ban on alcohol?" to "What is your favorite social media site?" These four questions received upwards of 150 comments each, representing a wide range of opinions.

Each morning, the Baghdad PAS Facebook Team would meet to discuss and debate the appropriate "Question of the Day." A scan of the morning newspapers, morning television news broadcasts, and international news helped guide the team in selecting an appropriate question for the day. "The Question of the Day" was posted by mid-morning and Baghdad PAS made every effort to post the questions at the same time, each day, establishing a pattern for the Embassy's Facebook community.

Increasing Frequency of Postings: Postings during Facebook's first half-year at Embassy Baghdad were sporadic at best. From 2010 to 2011, Baghdad PAS increased the frequency of postings, with new content added daily, in an effort to include two to four posts per day.

Expanded Arabic-language Engagement: Embassy Baghdad relied heavily on an American audience in the initial growth period of the site. In the summer of 2010, the page's focus was shifted to Iraqis as the primary audience and English-speaking Arabs with ties to Iraq as a secondary audience. By increasing the number of Arabic-language posts, PAS strengthened the dialogue between the Embassy and its fans, and increased the conversations between Arabic-speaking fans. Efforts to broaden Iraqi participation began in earnest in September 2010, with more frequent postings in Arabic, and the dedication of Arab staff to monitor comments and develop appropriate responses.

Attached to each posting in Arabic was the following sentence: "an English translation of this post can found in the first comment below."

By increasing the Arabic-language information on the site, a surprising development emerged. English-speaking/writing Iraqis who still wanted to engage in English (thereby using the Embassy's Facebook page as a English-language resource) responded to Arabic-language posts in English. Almost all threads of conversation were carried in both Arabic and English, with Baghdad PAS responding to fan comments and concerns in both Arabic and English.

Streamlining Facebook-by-Committee: Social media interaction must be timely. PAS eliminated the Facebook Committee and created a structure where the deputy public affairs officer, information officer, information resource officer, and assistant information officer for social media, and two locally engaged staff met weekly to discuss story/posting ideas. A smaller group composed of the information officer, assistant Information officer for social media, and one locally engaged staff (an Iraqi national) met each morning to review the Facebook goals for the day. By streamlining the process while still maintaining appropriate supervision, Baghdad PAS became more responsive to the Embassy's Facebook fan-base and consistently engaged in real-time. Topics for discussion were always presented in a neutral fashion, with the Embassy acting as the moderator and seldom offering opinions. While Baghdad PAS asked general questions about the current climate across the Middle East, conversations steered clear of controversial issues in Iraq and made no references to any government officials or political leaders in Iraq.

Giving a name and a face to the "Administrator": U.S. Embassies around the world are faced with the dilemma of using individual identities of Facebook Team members to engage foreign populations, or to use on the title of "Administrator" to engage. Given the need to establish a rapport with the Iraqi population in the wake the U.S. troop withdrawal, Baghdad PAS used a hybrid approach, responding as an "Administrator" to various questions (i.e., visa/consular questions, employment opportunities at the U.S. Embassy, etc.) but also responding to individual posts with the first names of some members of the Facebook Team. To give the Facebook community an opportunity to actually put a face to a name, Baghdad PAS posted pictures of the team; this received positive feedback in both English, and in Arabic.

The use of personal names and identities of individual Foreign Service officers and locally engaged staff creates an inherent challenge in an embassy like the U.S. Mission in Baghdad as turnover is high, and most Foreign Service assignments in Iraq are only one year. For many locally engaged staff, work at the American Embassy in Baghdad prevents myriad challenges. The threat from Iranian-backed militias, al-Qaeda in Iraq, and criminal syndicates that engage in kidnapping, extortion, and terrorism remain real concerns for the locally engaged staff of the U.S. Embassy.

U.S. Embassy Baghdad's Facebook
Team.June 2011

Methodology: YouTube's "Window into the Embassy" Series

In addition to the growing number of Iraqis on Facebook, YouTube emerged as another very popular social media platform from which Iraqis deliver information. Baghdad PAS had signed up for a YouTube site in early 2010, but had yet to brand the site in any measurable way.[6] In January 2010, Embassy PAS posted videos (in English) of various cultural events, including a volleyball match between a group of Embassy personnel and students from Baghdad University. While these videos received a few hits, interest in video content was sparse. In the fall of 2010, Baghdad PAS sought to leverage Iraqi interest in YouTube to increase the Embassy's online visual engagement with the people of Iraq. The Facebook Team (which, was soon renamed to be the "Social Media Team,") created an Arabic-language series of YouTube posts entitled "Window into the Embassy," geared toward explaining the U.S. civilian presence in Iraq. The concept of the series was simple: Arabic-speaking FSOs and development professionals working at the American Embassy (and at civilian-led American Provincial Reconstruction Teams around the country) would discuss in Arabic America's enduring civilian commitment to Iraq and its people, highlighting our mutual cooperation under the U.S.–Iraq Strategic Framework Agreement.

The initial episode outlined the series' premises and featured the Embassy's information officer, an Embassy political officer, consular officer, and cultural affairs officer.[7] The introductory episode received positive reviews from the Iraqi populace (and media) and was widely acknowledged by the Embassy Facebook community as an excellent outreach initiative. Baghdad PAS began to produce additional episodes, which responded to fan-feedback from the introductory video. Subsequent episodes featured officers who were proficient in the Iraqi dialect of Arabic[8] describing various aspects Embassy Baghdad's mission in furtherance of strengthening the bilateral relationship.

Baghdad PAS ensured that the video could be accessed on three distinct platforms: (1) the Embassy's Facebook page; (2) the Embassy's YouTube page; and (3) the Embassy's Web site. With assistance from the Department's Bureau of International Information Programs, videos for the series were also posted on the State Department's Arabic-language Web site, thereby receiving additional hits from across the region.[9]

The use of YouTube to further "humanize" the U.S. civilian presence was well received by the Iraqi populace and provided the Embassy with expanded opportunities to explain our civilian presence, publicize our mutual cooperation under the Strategic Framework Agreement, and familiarize the Iraqi public with the new civilian face of U.S. engagement. Additionally, the shelf life of YouTube is limitless, and videos recorded more than a year ago still continue to garner page views.

Results

U.S. Embassy Baghdad's Facebook revitalization resulted in a growing total fan-base, with an average of 100 new fans joining each week. The post's Facebook page currently holds the number-two spot in absolute numbers (behind the U.S. Embassy in Cairo) in the region for most fans on an Embassy Facebook page. Compared to Mission Morocco, a country with a similar size population but much higher Internet penetration rate, U.S. Embassy Baghdad's Facebook page has more than double the fan base. Embassy Baghdad's Facebook page has become an important, viable form of two-way communication between the American Embassy and Iraqi populace during a time in which security restrictions on movements outside the Embassy compound often hamper direct, face-to-face engagement. Responses to the "Question of the Day" initiative were immediate and positive, with posts routinely attracting over 100 responses and a spirited debate among fans. Indeed, Iraqis have often praised Embassy Baghdad's Facebook page for being "a place for real democratic dialogue."

The "Window on the Embassy" series has attracted nearly 53,000 views since its debut episode in late December 2010, and received positive coverage in Iraqi media and blogs. The initial Social Media Team attracted nearly 25,000 views in the first year of the page's existence, and the subsequent team continues this tradition of online engagement, expanding the content to include videos on employment at the American Embassy, and information on how to avoid visa scams.

Analysis

In addition to broadening the audience, the Facebook page gained credibility with fans by permitting alternative views and diminishing the impression of the page as USG propaganda. An important result of "The Question of the Day" initiative was increased insight into Iraqi society. For example, one "Question of the Day" revealed that the Facebook fan base trusts al-Hurra most among TV networks (44 percent of respondents), followed by BBC Arabic and al-Arabiya. Though not representative of all sectors of Iraqi society, the data provide feedback from a very important demographic—young, media-savvy Iraqis—and will assist USG messengers in selecting the appropriate networks for specific messages. Similarly, a question about which social networking sites are the most widely used in Iraq confirmed that Facebook is the hands-down favorite Web site for engagement. This was an important indicator with the rise of Twitter and a desire from the State Department for all posts to actively engage on Twitter. To date, Twitter's popularity in Iraq remains questionable, and Facebook and YouTube continue to retain the top social media slots in popularity.

Perhaps most important, audience growth and shift have bolstered the utility of Facebook as a mechanism for generating interest in exchange programs and scholarships, as well as a platform for messaging on USG objectives. Indeed, the Embassy witnessed a dramatic increase in the number of outstanding applicants for its programs, many of whom learned about the opportunities on Facebook. Education and study in the United States are two of the most frequent subjects of inquiry on Facebook, which led

PAS to develop a Facebook sister-site, StudyUSAIraq,[10] a more interactive page staffed by an American Educational Advisor dedicated to answering every inquiry in detail. StudyUSAIraq has enjoyed robust and consistent growth since its debut in late September 2010.

The work of Embassy Baghdad's YouTube channel is arguably Baghdad PAS' biggest social media success. While the numbers remain modest by international social media standards, the steady growth of Embassy Baghdad's YouTube presence in Iraq's social media landscape is an important development for the U.S. messaging efforts in Iraq. Baghdad PAS' insistence on making Arabic-language videos demonstrated an interest in the Arabic language and a respect for Iraqi culture. The inclusion of American faces to engage the Iraqi populace allowed the United States to "reintroduce" itself to the online community in Iraq. Rather than seeing video clips of uniformed U.S. military personnel in Iraq, the image and video of U.S. civilian personnel non-security and non-defense related concerns was a breath of fresh air for an Iraqi populace that yearned for a more organic relationship with the United States.

Conclusions and Recommendations

Social media engagement has become an integral part of U.S. Embassy outreach efforts throughout the world. These efforts have been particularly critical in Iraq, where the security environment does not permit the regular face-to-face interaction that is an integral part of any U.S. Embassy public diplomacy strategy. As with any communication with a foreign audience, there are risks. Some in the Iraqi Government, as in governments throughout the region, view Facebook with both reasonable and unreasonable suspicion. Iraqi youth and human rights activists used Facebook as an organizational tool in the lead-up to the February 25, 2011,

"Day of Rage" and in planning subsequent protests. PAS has been careful ensure our social media efforts remain "social," rather than political, and Embassy staff has briefed select representatives in the Government of Iraq on our intentions.

While the use of English-language outreach remains an important Public Diplomacy tool, it is critical that American Embassies in the Middle East and North Africa continue to engage their online communities in the local language. This will require additional resources, including social media-savvy State Department officers who also speak and read Arabic. Additional local staff may be required to ensure the Embassy is able to respond to postings, questions, and other inquiries, in real-time.

Successive generations of U.S. diplomats and development professionals in Iraq should continue to leverage social media to engage the Iraqi population, deliver key and targeted policy messages, and remind Iraqis of the shared interests by the two nations. Embassy Baghdad should devote American and locally engaged staff to continue social media engagement. A small, but agile team of both American and Iraqi Embassy personnel can have a huge impact on the U.S. ability to message the Iraqi populace using social media. Video content has provided the United States a successful tool of informing and should continue.

Notes

1. http://georgewbush-whitehouse.archives.gov/news/releases/2008/11/20081127-2.html
2. http://www.state.gov/r/.
3. http://unpan1.un.org/intradoc/groups/public/documents/dsg/unpan044212.pdf.

4. http://www.huffingtonpost.com/2010/01/21/baghdad-us-embassy-huntin_n_431728.html.
5. http://www.facebook.com/embassybaghdad.
6. http://www.youtube.com/user/usembassybaghdad.
7. http://www.youtube.com/watch?v=ynKe4OBuglo.
8. http://www.youtube.com/watch?v=5BY-tigDVDo.
9. Representatives from IIP indicated that the video was shared on a Moroccan news aggregator Web site, which generated additional traffic.
10. http://www.facebook.com/StudyUSAIraq.

Acknowledgments

Martin Quinn, Minister Counselor for Public Affairs, U.S. Embassy Baghdad

David Ranz, Deputy Public Affairs Officer, U.S. Embassy Baghdad

Stephen Stark, Assistant Information Officer for Social Media, U.S. Embassy Baghdad

Saher Al-Twal, Information Specialist, U.S. Embassy Baghdad

Hiba (*Family Name Withheld*), Information Assistant, U.S. Embassy Baghdad

The many Iraqi friends and fans of U.S. Embassy Baghdad's Facebook/YouTube pages

8

The Last Three Feet: Understanding What Pakistanis Are Saying

Walter Douglas

The U.S.–Pakistan relationship is one of the most important and most challenging in the world. The recent events that have shaped the relationship are too numerous to list. But they do continually lead both sides to examine the status of the relationship. Secretary Clinton recently stated:

> *[Pakistani] Foreign Minister Khar and I had a constructive discussion of our common concerns, from confronting violent extremism, to supporting Afghan-led reconciliation, to improving our bilateral relationship. Building and sustaining a relationship based on mutual interest and mutual respect takes constant care and work from both sides, from the daily engagements of our embassies to high-level meetings like the one we had today. Now, I am sure we will continue to have our ups and downs, but this relationship is simply too important to turn our back on it for both nations. And we both, therefore, remain committed to continue working to improve understanding and cooperation.[1]*

Supporting the relationship is a large American Embassy in Islamabad. Equally large, compared to similar programs in other countries, is its public diplomacy operation. Its mission is to reduce support for terrorist and other extremist groups and to deepen and broaden our relationship with the people of Pakistan. To do this, the educational and professional exchange programs for Pakistan are the largest in the world and the press section is on duty 24/7.

This paper looks at one aspect of public diplomacy in Pakistan. It is the story of how the American Embassy became better at understanding what was important to Pakistanis. It was crucial to being able to carry out the mission as stated above.

Communicating

Many communications specialists use a formula with four steps to describe their activity: (1) understand, (2) engage, (3) inform, and (4) influence. A lot of attention is given to steps two and three, hoping that they result in step four.

The least amount of attention is given to the first step, which is to understand what people are saying and thinking. Muslim populations are vocal in what is important to them. Yet these conversations are in their languages, not ours. Is this widely appreciated?

The Problem: Urdu (not English) is the National Language of Pakistan

In Pakistan, understanding the importance of these conversations means understanding the role of Urdu. The national debate takes place in the vernacular, not in English. Yet this is not captured in most Western material written about the country. Foreign experts on Pakistan rarely use vernacular sources, and the vernacular media are almost never *quote*d anywhere.

Why is this? Outside of Pakistan, there is a misconception that many Pakistanis speak English. Certainly, there is a vibrant English-speaking community in Pakistan, and foreigners generally restrict most of their interactions to this group. Pakistan also has well-written English-language media.[2] But after independence from Great Britain in 1947, Urdu became the national language and English usage began to wane.

The result is that today the English-language media is tiny and offers a misleading picture of Pakistan. It is almost all in print (particularly helpful for those living outside of the country), and with one minor TV station (rumored to be watched mostly by the diplomatic community). For newspapers, accurate readership information is not available. Estimates are that they reach no more than 100,000 people, accounting for only .01 percent of the media audience in Pakistan.

One Pakistani journalist explained to me that there are three types of media consumers in Pakistan. There are those who are internationally educated. There are those who are educated at universities within Pakistan. And then there are those with madrassa or other non-elite education. The English-language media appeals only to that first group. In a poor country like Pakistan, that is not large.

Furthermore, the English-language media especially targets those who live outside of Pakistan. The letters to the editor section reflects this, with heavy traffic from the diaspora, which has lost its Urdu. As one senior editor in Pakistan told me, "It's for you." In other words, the foreigners are the real consumers.

Too many officials outside of Pakistan do not understand the limited scope of English-language media. When I served in Pakistan, an official in Washington called up to ask what we were doing about an article that appeared in one of Pakistan's English-language newspapers. I responded, "Nothing; it hasn't appeared in the Pakistani press." The official quoted the English-language newspaper article, and I insisted that it had not appeared in the Pakistani media. I needed to explain that an English-language newspaper with a circulation of a few thousand readers was not a significant part of the Pakistani media, and only when a story appeared in the Urdu media would it be noteworthy. This story never did, and it died.

The flaw with relying on English-language media is that it reflects an elite, outside-looking viewpoint. The public diplomacy challenge was to develop a better sense of what was going on in Pakistan. To accomplish this, we turned to Urdu.

The Solution: Analyzing the Urdu Media

Understanding the influence of television was the first step. The illiteracy rate in Pakistan is at least 50 percent.[3] In addition, Pakistan tends to be more of an oral than a reading or written culture. As a result, television plays a major role in the day-to-day life of Pakistanis. The evening talk shows are probably the leading source of public opinion. Television is realistically the only way to reach a large percentage of the 180 million Pakistanis.

The Embassy decided to capture the Urdu environment by employing a new strategy—watching more television. Most of the talk shows aired at night, so we shifted the hours of some locally employed staff (LES) and hired additional ones. This allowed shifts to start at 3:00 in the afternoon and go into the night. These Pakistani colleagues would send us a topline report before going home. Of course, there were more shows and opinions aired each night than our night shift could monitor. We recorded these other programs and had our larger daytime press staff listen and deliver reports on items related to the United States.

The Embassy did not ignore traditional media. Urdu newspapers and the English-language press were also monitored. Nor did it ignore the nascent social media that exists in Pakistan. However, it allocated its resources based on the recognition that both outlets have only a limited audience and influence.

What did we do with this information from the Urdu media? At 8:30 each morning, our public diplomacy officers met with the press LES to discuss the stories of the past 24 hours. This discussion was not just a verbatim recitation of what was reported. We asked our LES to explain the political significance of the stories. We drilled them with questions when we saw something that needed deeper understanding. We also looked at the English-language media, and made startling observations about the difference in the reporting.

In 2012, the U.S.–Pakistan relationship experienced a number of stressful events. As the two countries lurched from crisis to crisis, the year offered an exceptional insight into the wide difference in coverage between the English and the Urdu media. The former—with all of their well-educated reporters who had been exposed to the West, including on American exchange programs—gave fairly straight coverage, with op-ed pages full of reasoned debate about how to improve the U.S.–Pakistan relationship.

This was not the case in the Urdu media, especially the talk shows. They were pumping aggressive nationalism and virulent condemnations of the United States. They found that the Pakistani military was always right. When some Pakistani journalists ventured to criticize the Pakistani military, they reversed course quickly.

It should also be noted that the two types of media granted different coverage to different stories. The Urdu media generally started with domestic stories. A change in the price of sugar or electricity had a tremendous impact on its less affluent audience. Many of these stories received much less coverage in the English-language media. Instead, international issues and the politics in the capital dominated headlines.

Following our 8:30 meeting in the Public Affairs Section, a small group of us went up to the ambassador's office to discuss the stories. In the room were not only the ambassador, but also the deputy charge of mission (the number two in an embassy), the political section chief, the economic section chief and a few other staffers working close to the ambassador. Here, we discussed the day's media and received insights from the ambassador and the rest on what some of the wider political implications were in the stories we reported on. This was one of the most insightful meetings in the Embassy, and it set the tone for the day's events.

Producing the Pakistan Media Analysis

For the Public Affairs Section, we now had the raw material to begin our daily media report. We called it the Pakistan Media Analysis, to emphasize that we were not just reporting on what the press said, but analyzing it. It is because of the analysis that it is available only to government officials.

This is where the time difference with Washington worked in our favor. (This is certainly not something we would say when we were on video conferences and telephone calls late at night.) One of the American officers in the Public Affairs Section would draft up the daily analysis. It usually consisted of a one-page summary of key stories and analysis, followed by two to four pages of verbatim reporting from television and print. We also included three or four cartoons from the newspapers.

The draft analysis was then reviewed and edited by others in the Public Affairs Section. From there, it was sent to offices in our government that deal with Pakistan and Afghanistan. Our goal was to have it in Washington offices by 7:00 AM each day. We almost always succeeded.

At first, we were surprised by its popularity. Officers from the Pakistan desk in the State Department started to mention it. Then we heard that the Pakistan team at the National Security Staff at the White House read it every morning. Congressional staffers began to hear about it, and we put them on our distribution list. New officers arriving at post mentioned its popularity in official Washington.

The Embassy's success relied on one key point. The focus of its analysis was always on the Urdu media, and especially on the television broadcasts that reached huge audiences. By not relying on the English language, we increased the American government's understanding of what was going on in Pakistan.

The Environment

When monitoring the Pakistan media, there is one point that always needs to be kept in mind. According to Freedom House, we are operating in a difficult environment. It ranks the Pakistani media as 144th out of 197 countries on its scale of press freedom (197 is the worst).[4]

Part of that ranking is influenced by the fact that Pakistan is the most dangerous country in the world for a journalist to work in. Last year, according to the Committee to Protect

Journalists, 8 Pakistani journalists were killed in the line of work between 2011 and 2012.[5]

This has an intimidating effect on the media. Since the government lifted some formal controls over the media under President Asif Zardari in 2008,[6] the Pakistani media has gained some privileges. It is even rambunctious at times. Nonetheless, it is still 144th out of 197. If you take away the journalists who were killed, the number would not be quite so low. But it still would be far from Western standards.

While the press may not be free, its reporting is invaluable. Because key Pakistani organizations use it to express their views, it is still the best window into what is going on in Pakistan.

The Importance of a Complete Public Diplomacy Program

The difficult environment presented another challenge: the Embassy could not rely on using the media to get out the American word. Every time we put information into the press, it could be smothered by countervailing stories. We recognized that while we needed to engage the Pakistani media, we needed to rely on wider public diplomacy activities to explain what we were doing in Pakistan.

In practice, educational and professional exchanges—the Fulbright scholarships and the International Visitors programs are the two leaders—combined with bringing in American speakers and cultural programs were equally important to media engagement. In fact, thanks to Congressional and USAID generosity, our exchange programs in Pakistan are the largest in the world. Public diplomacy is not just about the press. It is the sum of many parts that can communicate to a country.

Conclusion

English can be a pernicious influence. Many people in the target audience speak it. Most do not. It is important that every public diplomacy officer recognize its limitations, and use or find resources that can help understand what is going on in the vernacular. This is where the real stories lie.

Notes

1. Remarks by Secretary of State Clinton, "Press Availability on the London Conference," Foreign Commonwealth Office, London, United Kingdom, February 23, 2012. http://www.state.gov/secretary/rm/2012/02/184577.htm.
2. A few examples include *Dawn* (www.dawn.com), the *Daily Times* (www.dailytimes.com.pk), *The Nation* (www.nation.com.pk), the *Pakistan Observer* (www.pakobserver.net), and *The News International* (www.thenews.com.pk).
3. According to 2005 CIA estimates: total population: 49.9 percent, male: 63 percent, female: 36 percent. https://www.cia.gov/library/publications/the-world-factbook/geos/pk.html.
4. Karin Deutsch Karlekar and Jennifer Dunham, *Freedom of the Press 2012: Breakthroughs and Pushback in the Middle East.* Freedom House, Press Freedom Index: 2012. http://www.freedomhouse.org/sites/default/files/Booklet%20for%20Website.pdf.
5. Committee to Protect Journalists, "Pakistan," 2011.http://cpj.org/killed/2011/; 2012: http://cpj.org/killed/2012/.
6. Marco Mezzera and Safdar Sial. "Media and Governance in Pakistan: A Controversial yet Essential Relationship." IFP Democratisation and Transitional Justice Cluster, Country Case Study, October 2010. http://www.initiativeforpeacebuilding.eu/pdf/pakistanOct.pdf, pp. 8, 10.

Successful Public Diplomacy Officers in The Future

Bruce Wharton

Successful public diplomacy officers (PDOs) have always needed a detailed knowledge of the tools and programs the U.S. government uses to understand, engage, inform, and influence foreign publics. They have also needed excellent management, communications, and interpersonal skills, and the ability to listen to and learn from the people of the countries in which they serve. This last element is vital: Good PDOs must find productive common ground with people from cultures and histories that are not like ours. Great PDOs use that understanding to inform our policies and shape our programs.

In the coming years, successful PDOs will add some new capabilities to the knowledge and skills of their predecessors. Among those new abilities, the following are likely to be important.

They will be strong leaders and managers in the interagency environment. As more U.S. agencies establish presences abroad—40 now have representatives overseas—and U.S. Embassies expand to host them, PDOs will need to create and manage a coherent public image. They must forge a real "e pluribus unum" in the way foreign publics perceive the U.S. government's policies and programs. To do that, to imagine and build an answer to the core question of "What image does the Embassy want to convey to local citizens?" will require interagency leadership. Public diplomacy officers who can gain the support of the ambassador and the deputy chief of mission for an embassy-wide PD program under the leadership of the public affairs officer (PAO) will have an advantage in this complex challenge.

Here's an example of how it can work: In 2009, the PAO in Kampala pioneered what we now call the Kampala Model. In this model, all agencies are entitled to PD support, and all agencies are expected to follow the PAO's lead on engagement with host country publics. There is a parallel expectation that the agencies receiving public affairs and public diplomacy support from the PAO will also contribute resources to the effort. There are many forms that support can assume. In Kampala it included cost-sharing for some public programs, technical support provided episodically, and long-term seconding of staff to the PD office. Strong PD leadership ensures that foreign publics receive consistent information about the United States and that programs such as Embassy Kampala's quiz show-based, national HIV/AIDS education campaign are stronger and more successful.

They will be social entrepreneurs. Public diplomacy officers will make strategic use of an embassy's convening power to create partnerships with people and institutions in ways that serve our mutual interests and stretch resources. Example: In 2010, the Bureau of African Affairs worked closely with colleagues in the Department of State, including the special advisor on information technology and the under secretary for public diplomacy and public affairs, and with the U.S. Embassy in Kenya and a consortium of

African information technology NGOs to establish a program called "Apps4Africa." This contest-driven initiative convened East Africa's information technology developers and civil society leaders to explore cooperation on pressing social needs and develop IT responses to those needs. The responses were in the form of applications, or "apps," that work on cell phones or computers and provide some socially or developmentally useful tool for no-cost use by people in the region. The U.S. contribution was modest, consisting of conceptualization, invitations to key organizations, and about $50,000 in funding for advertising, organizational support, and independent judging. The resulting contest boosted tech development in East Africa, brought disparate groups together for the first time, and led to several useful applications. The winner was "iCow," a cell phone-based app that helps farmers better manage the breeding cycles of their cattle. Prosaic, perhaps, but vitally important to rural development in a part of the world where cattle are both sustenance and wealth. The Apps4Africa program is now being replicated in other parts of Africa to develop practical responses and adaptations to climate change. In these initiatives, the U.S. government imprint is light, and our partners do most of the organizational and promotional work. But the results— stronger institutions, new economic opportunities, development support, and identifying African solutions to African challenges—are all in line with U.S. policy in the region. Further, this program has won the U.S. government credit and goodwill with influential technology and development communities in Africa and the United States.

Another example: In 2011, our PAO in Harare used U.S.–branded technology—the Kindle—and a partnership with the U.S. Chautauqua Institution to attract influential Zimbabweans to an Embassy-hosted reading club that includes participants from diverse social sectors and political backgrounds. In discussing books from the Chautauqua list, people who would not otherwise meet get to know one other and consider common interests and concerns, building a foundation for the social and political comity Zimbabwe needs. The PAO's role was to bring these diverse opinion leaders together in an interesting and neutral space. Convening people who might not otherwise meet to explore common concerns and seek cooperative responses to those concerns is social entrepreneurism. It is a low-cost, infinitely flexible form of smart power, one that successful PDOs will use increasingly in the future. It respects the value of finding local solutions for local problems and addresses our need to work effectively within financial constraints.

They will be savvy about the effective use of technology and social media. Successful PDOs will understand that these new technologies are the means to an end, not the end itself. They will develop effective ways to use these tools to advance foreign knowledge of the United States and our knowledge of foreign communities. For example, our press officer in Pretoria used the South African "MXit" platform, the text message-based social media platform most popular among South African youth, to invite people to "Ask President Obama a Question" just before the president's 2009 travel to Ghana. Over 300,000 responses in three days drew enormous attention to the president's travel and the major policy address he delivered before the Ghanaian parliament. Just as important, the questions asked via MXit provided insight into young Africans' concerns and opinions, allowing our responses to address those specific interests. This dialogue helped create positive new connections and understanding between the U.S. and African youth. Our PD office in South Africa has also developed expertise in using Twitter to inform local and regional media of U.S. policy issues. In a July 2011 article about government use of social media, *Foreign Policy* magazine wrote this: "Interested in Africa? Probably the best 'follow' is the U.S. Embassy in South Africa (@USEmbPretoria), whose wide-ranging feed is a model of good Twitter etiquette and '21st-century diplomacy.'"

Another example: In 2010, our PAO in Guinea combined cell phone text messaging with the Ushahidi on-line mapping platform and the star power of Miss Guinea to create a citizen-driven election observation effort for Guinea's first elections. The PAO and Embassy worked with local phone companies to get a short number to which Guineans could text messages about how voting and related administrative and security issues were proceeding on election day. He also worked with the Ushahidi NGO to have the information sent in by Guineans entered and plotted on the Ushahidi Web site in real time. This gave citizens, journalists, elections officials and observers an almost immediate geographic view of where things were going well and where attention was needed. And, the PAO persuaded Miss Guinea 2010 to produce TV, radio, and print media ads to let the people of Guinea know about the system and encourage their participation. While not up to Carter Center standards for observing elections, this program let Guineans know that the United States was interested and paying attention, and it gave them a sense of confidence in and ownership of this first real election in the country's 52 years of independence.

They will be strategic thinkers and planners, and fully conversant in policy. The next generation of successful PDOs will make PD programs such a natural and integral part of an embassy's exercise of smart power that we will stop thinking about public diplomacy as a separate diplomatic function. They will understand policy and how host nation publics will perceive it, and use that knowledge to help make policy and programs more effective. They will put policy at the center of public diplomacy and will be so conversant in it that other embassy officers will seek their advice on how to better achieve U.S. policy goals in that country. These successful PDOs will also help their colleagues serving in other parts of the embassy become more effective communicators and public diplomats themselves. Just as public diplomacy officers must understand and work to support U.S. policy, other embassy officers must understand that public diplomacy is a great deal more than press releases and speeches, and that they also have a role to play in engaging foreign publics. Our PAO in South Africa is a good example of a PD officer who brings policy and public diplomacy together effectively throughout the embassy's work. He is in at the beginning, middle, and end of every public event the embassy does, and often serves as the acting DCM or Charge.

They just won't give up. Finally, the successful PD officer of the future will be a bit like the title character in Kipling's short story "The Elephant's Child." Like the young elephant, they will have insatiable curiosities and will be willing to ask the most challenging and dangerous questions. Where the elephant's child asked questions such as "What does the crocodile eat for dinner?" successful PDOs will ask "What do our audiences expect of us?" and "What is our policy objective here?" And, like the elephant's child, in pursuing the answers to those questions, they will discover and acquire new abilities and will become more capable leaders of our absolutely vital engagement with those whose cultures and histories are not just like ours.

10

Conclusions

William P. Kiehl

What have we learned from the foregoing case studies? What lessons can be drawn from these examples? What do these stories tell us about the art of public diplomacy?

In examining these contemporary case studies along with the interviews in appendix 1 and comparing them with examples of successful public diplomacy cases from the pre-USIA consolidation era, one can see some clear similarities despite the obvious differences in today's public diplomacy climate. The end of the Cold War and the beginnings of the Age of Terrorism, the 24/7 news cycle and the Internet, and organizational changes within the PD structure have all had far reaching effects yet the successful art of public diplomacy still rests on three easily identifiable pillars.

Commonality

The Public Affairs Section must identify that which is important to both the host nation and the United States and amplify that common interest. That which is important to the United States but not to the host country or vice versa is a weak reed upon which to base a public diplomacy program. This may appear obvious, but one sees too many examples of such misguided efforts, usually directed from

Washington and forced on the field that it may not be so obvious after all. This leads directly to the second pillar.

Field Driven

American and locally employed staff members at U.S. embassies and consulates live and work in the local environment and should know best what the host nation is thinking. Why not let the field post drive the process rather than leave it to the massive bureaucracy in Washington that may have the financial resources but not the knowledge of how best to apply them. When creative and knowledgeable field posts drive the process there is a much greater chance of success. The cookie-cutter, one size fits all prescriptions from headquarters rarely hit the mark.

Local Resources

Field posts need not solely depend upon resources from Washington headquarters to effect positive change and initiate effective public diplomacy programs. Careful planning and imagination can provide a myriad of local, home grown resources and private-public partnerships to bring those resources to bear without having to rely on Washington funding and the "strings" that often accompany it.

Certainly Washington headquarters has an important role in prioritizing overall efforts and crafting overarching themes. Efficiencies are often achieved through pooling resources and duplicating successful efforts from one country and "grafting" them onto another country's programs. But an over-reliance on Washington and/or Washington-centered micro-management of public diplomacy usually does far more harm than good. Successful PD campaigns usually have a mix of locally resourced, field-driven, commonality-focused programs with a minimum of interference from headquarters. If there is a lesson, this is it.

Appendix 1. Interviews with Public Diplomacy Practitioners at Overseas Posts

Gloria Berbena, Counselor of Public Affairs,U.S. Interests Section, Havana, Cuba

Q: Our guest today is Ms. Gloria Berbena, who is the counselor of public affairs in the U.S. Interests Section in Havana, Cuba. First of all, we have an interests section and not an embassy, and you might want to mention that. But given the difficult political environment facing the interest section in Havana, what kind of programing can you undertake, and how is that program linked to the accomplishment of U.S. government objectives in Cuba?

GLORIA BERBENA: Right. Well, as you know, we don't have full diplomatic relations between the U.S. government and the Cuban government. Cuba also has the lowest level of connectivity in the Western Hemisphere. We have a long and troubled and complex history with Cuba. All of that combines to make for a really challenging public diplomacy environment. But that being said, we are very clear about our priorities—our public diplomacy priorities in Cuba.

First, of course, is to advance U.S. national interests. Second, of course, is to support the Cuban people in achieving their personal destiny, and then supporting the free flow of information to, from and within Cuba. And all of our programming in Cuba is driven by those guiding priorities. And even though we work within a constrained environment, we're actually able to do quite a bit.

We reach out to a broad spectrum of Cuban contacts in the cultural sector, academic sector, and religious groups. We try to do what we can with Cuban government officials and institutional representatives. Those, of course, are a little bit more difficult to reach, but we make our best effort.

Q: Could you say something about the audience—a little more about the audience with whom you deal and what sorts of groups or institutions do they belong to? And can you mention one or two specific activities that were particularly effective in getting your message across the Cuban community?

MS. BERBENA: No, happy to. Well, again, as I'd mentioned, we reach or try to reach the full spectrum of Cuban contacts. We're particularly successful with Cuban cultural contacts, civil society, of course; academics, to a limited extent. Less successful with student groups—that tends to be a group that's difficult for us to reach because they are more under Cuban control—Cuban government control. Doesn't mean that there's a lack of interest on their part at all, but it does mean that it's more of a challenge for us to connect with them.

But we have a number of programs despite the constrained environment that I think have been really successful. We run on-site information resource centers, which provides free Internet access to the Cuban public—uncensored access; distance—a variety of distance learning programs; a couple of examples: on independent journalism, journalistic practices, on information technology, on leadership programs. We offer courses on blogging, on basic computer technology, English teaching.

We work with new media to the extent that we can. Again, the connectivity issues in Cuba make it difficult because most Cubans aren't connected to the Internet. But we run a Facebook page, we have Web sites, we use SMS and Twitter to a certain extent, and we work with Cubans—the small but growing group of Cuban bloggers—Yoani Sanchez, for instance, is a very prominent example. But there are others as well who are trying to do the most that they can with the limited connectivity that's available in Cuba. And that's growing and we support them in every way that we can.

Q: You described this a little, about the new media and social media and the connectivity issue along with the political issue. The subject matter they deal with—you mention someone who's—deal a lot with human rights. Are—is there other subject matter that some of these bloggers deal with which is of interest to us (and ?) our priorities?

MS. BERBENA: Well, absolutely. Because information is so limited coming to and from the island, and because Cubans have such limited access to information, they're hungry for information coming in. I think the rest of the world is interested in what's going on in Cuba. So many of these bloggers, many of these independent journalists that we work with, many of the human rights activists are reporting on everyday conditions. What—how does the average Cuban live? What do they face? How does the society work, or not work, as the case may be? There is such a constrained information environment in Cuba that we spend a great deal of time just helping Cubans connect with each other and with the outside world. They are hungry for that information and we help them to connect in every way that we can.

Q: Good. Well, our thanks to Ms. Gloria Berbena, the counselor for public affairs in the U.S. Interests Section in Havana. The date is September 19th, 2011. This was recorded at George Washington University. Thank you very much for joining us.

MS. BERBENA: Thank you, my pleasure.

John Beyrle, Ambassador, U.S. Embassy, Moscow, Russia

ZSOFIA BUDAI: Hello and greetings from Moscow. My name is Zsofia Budai, and I am a deputy press attaché here. Today I have the honor of introducing to you Ambassador John Beyrle, our current Ambassador to the Russian Federation. Welcome, Ambassador Beyrle.

I'd like to tell you a little bit about his career before we get started. Ambassador Beyrle joined the State Department in 1983 and since then, he has held a variety of postings, both domestically and overseas. He has focused mainly on the former Soviet Union and Central and Eastern Europe. Prior to becoming ambassador to Russia in summer of 2008, he was ambassador to Bulgaria, and he also served two previous tours here in Moscow. Thus, Ambassador Beyrle has really a wealth of experience in Russia—he was even a student here in the 1970s—and he is very much in tune with what the Russian public knows about our public diplomacy initiatives.

With that, Ambassador Beyrle, I'd like to get started. First of all, I'd like to ask you a little bit about your role in promoting our public diplomacy initiatives as the ambassador. What is the specific role that you play in promoting public diplomacy here?

AMBASSADOR JOHN BEYRL: First of all, thanks very much for the opportunity to talk to you and to talk to people back in Washington.

When you talked about my bio, you started me out as a Foreign Service officer in 1983—that's absolutely correct, but actually before that, for five years, starting in 1977, I actually worked for the U.S. Information Agency overseas on American exhibitions that traveled around the Soviet Union. And I also worked at Voice of America for two years immediately before I joined the Foreign Service. So, for me, public diplomacy is kind of in the blood. My wife, Jocelyn Greene, is also a PD officer. So you ask, what's the role of an ambassador in terms of public diplomacy, it's something that's almost very personal for me. Here in Moscow, what we try to do—Jocelyn and I try to do in particular together—is host a lot of events at our residence, Spaso House. We do a lot of cultural concerts, both with American artists who are visiting, but also with Russian artists as well who have some sort of connection to America—either they play jazz, or they've just recently returned from a tour of the U.S., and we find that's a very good way to reach an audience that's right there in the house to show how much we value culture as part of public diplomacy outreach.

Beyond that, I have a blog now that we spend a lot of time putting together. When I travel out to the regions, I find that to be a very good way to reach the Russian people directly with the sorts of messages that we want to get out to them about what really unites the United States and Russia these days. What's interesting about the blog is, in addition to being on transmit, it's also an opportunity for me to be on receive, because I spend a lot of time in the evenings reading through the reactions to the blog. When I do a blog posting sometimes I'll get between 15 and 150 responses. I can't respond to them all, obviously, and some of them are kind of wacky, but a lot of them just give me a sense of what the average Russian thinks and how he or she responds to what the American ambassador has to say. And that really helps me a lot—helps us a lot here—to kind of hone the message a little bit better.

I do a lot of public speaking, obviously, when I travel, especially out to the provinces, which I try to do five, six, seven times a year. I go to universities and speak to student groups, and I try to always do that in a setting where I've got a chance to do more Q&A, which again for me is a kind of feedback loop, which is important.

And finally there are the traditional interviews. But not just interviews with the main television news programs or newspapers. We also try to broaden out a little bit here, because there is such a wealth of media out there. Not just social media, but I'm talking about new newspapers, new magazines, online journals. We try to reach different and broader audiences. I'll give you one example: I'm doing something with GQ next week. Why GQ? Because GQ, for some odd reason, good marketing I guess, has a very broad and interesting audience here. It's just a good way to reach people with the basic message. And the basic message is: Americans and Russians working together get a lot more done than when we are working separately or working against each other. It's really just that simple.

Mr. BUDAI: So based on your experiences giving interviews, talking to students, writing your blog, what are some of the major challenges that we face when it comes to public diplomacy in Russia?

AMB. BEYRLE: First, I really have to say that the environment is pretty welcoming. We have a lot of access here—I don't have any trouble getting on the radio, into the major newspapers with interviews. Part of this is a function of the reset. I think it's gotten a lot easier under the Obama Administration, since the first meetings between Obama and Medvedev, the relationship has improved a lot. At the same time, obviously; there are obstacles; there are challenges. One of the biggest challenges is that we are just not the only voice out there. And especially on state-run media, there's still a lot of active anti-American ideology that's being spread out there. I can go on TV and talk about the importance of the tenth anniversary of 9/11 and how it's brought America and Russia closer together on the anti-terrorism front, but if that same evening—as happened—Channel One television runs a news story in which they give a lot of credence to the "truther agenda," that special services in America actually sent the planes into the Twin Towers, suddenly you're right back where you started. So that's a big challenge.

Another challenge is just how dynamic the media environment is here and especially social and new media, which we spend a lot of time trying to track, and just trying to keep track of what the best inputs and outlets for us are. It's just a constantly shifting scene and I think we need to stay light on our feet to make sure that we're finding the best avenues for getting our message out.

And last I'd say just the size of the country. I mean, this is a country of nine time zones, 150–140 million people spread out. You can't really do it on a retail basis. I mean, you can, and when I travel I try to talk to students at universities. But a lot of it you really have to strategize on how you reach those parts of the country that otherwise aren't reached by our message at all.

Mr. BUDAI: So all of these public diplomacy initiatives that you undertake—what are you trying to achieve with them? What are Embassy Moscow's goals with public diplomacy?

AMB. BEYRLE: The meta-goal is to un-demonize the United States, because there's an interesting paradox. If you look at the public opinion polls here, there's been a remarkable shift just over the last three years. When I got here as ambassador in July of 2008, by November of 2008—which was kind of the low watermark—only 28 percent of Russians had a positive view of the United States. Now that figure is somewhere between 50 percent and 60 percent, which is very good. That means people think positively about the United States. But at the same time, that same group of people believes that this country, which they have a generally positive view of, somehow has negative motivations towards Russia. That we want to undermine Russia, that we want Russia to be a weak country. So we spend a lot of time trying to explain to Russians why that's not so, why we in America need Russia to be a strong country, to be a partner to the bigger challenges that we face in the 21st century.

And we go about that in a lot of different ways. I'd say probably on the media front first, we do try to reach new audiences. You're not going to change a lot of minds of people who are in their 50s, 60s, and 70s, who grew up during the Cold War. A lot of those people obviously are in positions of power. But you've got a new generation coming up which gets most of its news from the Internet, from Facebook, and we strategize a lot about how to reach those people.

On the educational side, traditionally educational exchanges have been a good way for us to promote better understanding, and what we're doing now is trying to broaden the university partnerships that already exist, many of which have spring up organically, without any help from the U.S. government at all, and just create a better environment for those sorts of partnerships to grow, to develop and expand. On the cultural front—also traditionally a good avenue for us to break down the barriers and the stereotypes—we're reaching out to different cultural media now. It's not just about jazz and classical music.

We've brought bluegrass to Russia; we had the first ever hip hop concert at Spaso House a few months ago with tremendous turnout of people that I'd never seen in the American ambassador's residence before. We are bringing contemporary theater here, doing exchanges between theater students in the United States and Russia. On the cultural side, we're really trying to broaden out beyond the traditional avenues that we've been in.

And sports I would point to also as kind of an offshoot of that, but really sports has become almost its own branch now. Through the Bilateral Presidential Commission, which has a working group devoted to culture, to sports, to media, we've really been successful in building some close partnerships between youth sports teams in areas like hockey and basketball, which are big in both countries. So it's a really rich agenda. As you know, we spend a lot of our time just trying to be as effective and as efficient as possible, because there are so many opportunities out there, you really have to choose them as carefully as you can.

Mr. BUDAI: And on the cultural front, we just launched American Seasons this past summer, correct?

AMB. BEYRLE: Yes, the American Seasons is kind of a riff on the old idea that you have the year of America in Russia and the year of Russia in America—a sort of traditional way of thinking about cultural exchange that the Russians understand. But we didn't want to limit it to just a year. So we came up with the idea of calling it the Seasons of America in Russia, which allows us to stretch it out a little bit. It also pays a little bit of homage to Sergei Diaghilev and what he did—the seasons of Russia in Europe in the last century. And under that, and by raising a lot of money from American companies, which we're much freer to do than we used to be when I started in this, we've been able to sponsor a lot of musical, theater, and dance groups here, starting with Alvin Ailey just a few months ago, which played to sold out audiences, and culminating with the Chicago Symphony Orchestra, which is going to do a tour in Russia next year, and that will be the first time we've had a major American symphony orchestra in about 10 or 15 years, I think. Together with that, as I mentioned, bluegrass, zydeco, contemporary theater exchanges, all sorts of things. It's a very exciting palate.

Mr. BUDAI: It is. Earlier you mentioned that you have a blog, and you also spoke about how important it is for us to be plugged into social media, because many Russians get their news online. Could you talk a little bit about Embassy Moscow's social media efforts? What's out there?

AMB. BEYRLE: Yes, we spend a lot of time on this because as I said, it's a way to reach an audience through no filters at all, and a new audience which sometimes is not as favorably disposed towards the United States as we would like. There's a kind of false perception out there that the young generation understands what America is about. Some of the biggest misperceptions we have come from young people, so reaching out through social media is really important. We've got two or three people on staff here who spend their time doing nothing but social media, both in terms of monitoring what's happening out there, and also finding ways for us to insert ourselves.

It's important because social media has just exploded in Russia over the last two or three years. I think only Israel has more hours by average citizen spent on social media than Russia. They spend double the amount of time on Facebook, on Twitter, on other social networking sites than Americans do. And this is a very free area right now. There's no censorship of the Internet to speak of in

Russia— certainly nothing compared to what we see in China. So it's a great opportunity for us. Also, Internet penetration is going way up. If you consider Internet penetration to encompass mobile penetration—most Russians now have cell phones, most of those are 3G and 4G—there's a great 4G network in Moscow, in St. Petersburg, several other big cities—so people who have a cell phone are plugged into the Internet.By those measures, Internet penetration is up to 80 percent, 85 percent in the big cities. So we've got to spend time thinking about how we tap into that to basically get a message across. It's nothing different from what we were doing when I was here with the traveling exhibits in the 1970s. We had a message that we were trying to get across in those days too, and we found that the most effective way in those days to do it was through these exhibits because we had no access to media to speak of. Now it's a very different story. The media is really now where it's at, especially social media. But it means that we've got to be a lot smarter, resources being strained as they always are, to get the most out of the money we put into it.

Mr. BUDAI: One final question. How have all of your experiences in Russia, especially as an ambassador for the past three, three and a half years, affected your views on public diplomacy in general?

AMB. BEYRLE: I'd go back a lot farther than just three, three and a half years as ambassador here. Going back to the first time when I was a student in the 70s, and especially that really formative experience working as a guide on American exhibitions in the 70s. It really taught me that alongside all of the hypocrisy and doubt and suspicions that Russians have towards the United States, there's still a real fascination and admiration for the United States. And that really hasn't changed over the years. Now Russians are able to act on it much more directly than before. We've given out more visas to Russians over the last two years than ever before, and we're going to break another record this year, I think. So understanding that even though there's still a lot of negative stereotyping, a lot of Cold War legacy that needs to be overcome, basically we're dealing with a Russian populace which is inclined to look at us in a favorable light, and believes that it's possible to have a partnership with the United States, that the United States is not fated to be an enemy or an adversary of Russia. With that as your basic foundational understanding, building public diplomacy, building outreach on top of that, can, I think be done a lot more effectively than if you somehow misperceive that reality.

Mr. BUDAI: Thank you very much for sharing your thoughts and experience, Ambassador Beyrle.

AMB. BEYRLE: My pleasure.

Atim Eneida George, Public Affairs Officer, U.S. Embassy, Nigeria

ATIM ENEIDA GEORGE: We hear so much about the brain drain. Career Connect was born of this commitment to the brain gain to actually encourage young people with global skills to return to their country of origin, see it as a land of opportunity and go about developing their own country.

It's an initiative that came from Nigerian colleagues at the U.S. consulate general in Lagos. We identified a cohort of nine students who were part of the educational advising center to become summer interns.

This is something I described as a win-win-win proposition. Students who were returning from studies in the United States had something meaningful to do during their summer break. Parents who were missing their children, their sons and daughters who'd studied in the United States got their kids home for the summer, and prospective employers had an opportunity to actually test young workers in their workplace.

One thing that I can tell you that really impressed me about the Career Connect was the network of students who had gone through our educational advising program and Career Connect and who were returning to take their place in industry and government and essentially in the private sector in Nigeria. And they're beginning to put together a network to open up the doors of opportunity to others.

We've had students who have worked at Coca-Cola, Nigeria breweries and UPS. Cisco Systems, which is operating in Nigeria, had recruited a person who had gone through our educational advising center, and she opened up the door for several others to get interviews with Cisco.

The whole question of what Nigerian students can learn from the U.S. work ethic is a very important one—one, because we stress critical thinking in the United States. We also value pragmatism and problem solving. And I think those are the kinds of lessons, you know, that Nigerian students would bring back. So rather than just see a problem and allow it to fester, I think a Nigerian student educated in the United States would set about problem-solving and would demonstrate the sort of proactive approach that one educated here would pursue, and that's a real benefit.

Gabriel Kaypaghian, Public Affairs Officer,U.S. Embassy, Mexico City, Mexico

Q: This video is being recorded at George Washington University. Today's date is October 13th, 2011. This video will be shown at the forum entitled: The Last Three Feet: New Media, New Approaches and New Challenges for American Public Diplomacy, which is being sponsored by the Institute for Public Diplomacy and Global Communication at George Washington University and the Public Diplomacy Council.

My guest today is Gabriel Kaypaghian, who up until recently was based at the American Embassy in Mexico. Thank you for being with us. My first question is that you were involved in a very interesting program there called Youth in Action. Can you tell me a little bit about the program and what we were trying to achieve with it?

GABRIEL KAYPAGHIAN: Sure. Thank you for giving us the opportunity to talk about this program. The name of the program in Spanish is "Jovenes en Accion" or Youth in Action. It was—it's a program that we initiated in 2010. It is somewhat unique because it's an exchange program that is co- sponsored by the Mexican government, the secretary of education and private sector partners, along with the Embassy in Mexico City.

The program reaches out to public school high school students, ages 14 to about 18 years old, and brings them to the United States for a five-week period during which they get instruction in leadership, English language skills. They also have a two-week stay with a family in the United States, which includes community service projects. And, during the same time, they develop a project, which they take back to Mexico to implement in their communities.

Q: Very interesting. Why the focus on youth in Mexico?

MR. KAYPAGHIAN: As many of you know, Mexico is going through some difficult times currently, with a lot of violence, especially as in relation to the drug cartel activity. One of the draws, obviously, of this situation is for youth to get involved in activities that lead to nowhere.

And through this program, and since we are approaching students who would be susceptible to this kind of draw, we hope to give them alternatives and teach them that they have the power to be leaders, to make changes in their communities and to help their community members to act and hopefully change and make their societies stronger and more resilient to these forces.

Q: Very interesting. What challenges, if any, did you face in identifying the proper candidates? And were they from all over the country?

MR. KAYPAGHIAN: Yeah. The first round of this program, which was in 2010 as I mentioned, had 50 students from all over the—all over Mexico. The second round, which was just this summer, has 68 students from 14 different states in Mexico. The students are organized into different teams. And the selection process for the students was based on, one, the fact that they had already shown some leadership qualities in their communities and their schools; two, that they had to come up with an actual proposal of what they wanted to do when they returned to Mexico; and three, that they had some English proficiency so that we weren't starting from zero.

As word is spreading of this program it's becoming easier to identify such students. Some of the challenges, obviously, are finding students who have the English language skills to be able to participate effectively. And other than that, there's been a very, very good response. There were more than 400 candidates who applied for this last round, of which 68 were chosen.

Q: I know it's early in the—in the process, but how would you rate the effectiveness of the efforts, and what kind of metrics do you think we could use to judge the effectiveness of the program?

MR. KAYPAGHIAN: Well, the idea of the program is develop a cadre of young leaders who, as they go into college and start their careers in whatever field it may be, they maintain this idea of empowerment, of civil society participation, and leadership. As you mentioned, we've only been—it's only been the second year, so some—the kids from the previous year, just a few of them are probably just starting out in college. So we'll still need to see the actual results at the end in a few more years.

However, the fact that the Mexican government is a sponsor, that there's private-sector involvement, ensures that their—the stakeholders, Mexican stakeholders—are interested in the success of these students and in their ability to be leaders and to actively promote change and greater safety and resiliency in their communities. So hopefully once this program continues, we'll have a very large number of students who will be networked, who will be continued—continually assisted by the State Department and by their local communities and by the other stakeholders so that they can actively promote change and ensure that their communities become safer and better places.

Q: What were their views of the United States?

MR. KAYPAGHIAN: I think a lot of students—and in fact, the last part of the program is that they spend one week here in Washington meeting with folks on the Hill and with people at the State Department. And they have a closing ceremony which is when I get the chance to meet them. And that's in fact one of the first questions I ask all of them, is what is your—what is your perception of the United States, how has it changed, and so on.

And interestingly these—a lot of these kids are kids who have not been really out of their communities, let alone out of Mexico. And they arrived in the United States with, you know, stereotypes of what Americans are like, of what America is all about. And it seems that a lot of them went back home very changed, especially because they actually spent time in communities with families and came to see that we have a lot more in common than they thought we did, and that everybody is concerned about, you know, what's happening in Mexico, what's happening in the border, how it affects the United States, how it affects their communities.

And the idea, and I think what a lot of them are walking away with, is that we're all in this together. It's a team effort. We all want to improve the situation for citizens, both in the United States and in Mexico. And most importantly: that they have the power; and they have the ability; and they can develop the skills to affect positive change.

Q: Thank you very much.

MR. KAYPAGHIAN: My pleasure.

Matt Lussenhop, Public Affairs Officer, U.S. Embassy, Kabul, Afghanistan

JIM KELMAN: This video is being recorded at George Washington University in Washington, DC. Today's date is October 13th, 2011.

My guest today is Matt Lussenhop who, until recently, was the American public affairs officer at the U.S. Embassy in Kabul, Afghanistan.

Matt, how do you assess running a public diplomacy program in a war zone? And how do you feel that we have been able to reach our audiences and for that matter, who are our audiences?

MATT LUSSENHOP: Well, to start with the first, our audiences in Afghanistan included the broad mass of Afghan public, many of whom are illiterate. So we often used radio, television as ways of getting our message out— and then, to be more specific, was young people, college students, university students, high school students, opinion leaders and influencers, including, you know, commentators and analysts of politics and so forth from the universities. So in many ways it's similar to what most public diplomacy operations do in the field. I mean, we had a broad audience, but also a segmented audience of key opinion leaders and sort of key sectors of society that were going to be increasingly important in the country.

And yeah, in a conflict zone like Afghanistan, you have a lot of constraints on what you can do, mostly because of security. But that said, we were still able to get out and do traditional public diplomacy, meaning just people-to-people, talking with people, talking to students, talking to university professors, talking to journalists, hearing their ideas, doing a lot of active listening for what were some of the issues and themes that they were interested in and concerned about and less of the, say, social diplomacy, you know, receptions, dinners, having coffee or going out to a restaurant with people. That was more difficult if not impossible, but the key element of getting outside the wire, outside the Embassy, in Afghan institutions and ministries and universities and schools and NGOs, we could do and— with some risk, more risk than, you know, many other places, but it was—you can't do public diplomacy if you are unable to do that.

MR. KELMAN: How did you break down your efforts? The traditional elements of public diplomacy, as you—as you just discussed, but a typical public diplomacy program involves exchanges; it involves press; it involves new media. It involves explaining U.S. policies to audiences in a way as to hopefully gain some understanding and even support for them.

MR. LUSSENHOP: I'd say, you know, we broke our activities into four broad goals of countering extremist voices, strengthening people-to-people ties, helping build Afghan communications capacities, both human and infrastructure, and expanding media outreach and getting our message out to a broader audience.

We used all the traditional tools of exchange programs: academic exchange, professional exchanges. Afghanistan, you know, despite 30 years of war and an ongoing insurgency, has some very strong and thriving institutions; has a cultural and educational tradition; has a, you know, very active media. So we had a lot of great interlocutors and contacts and audiences.

Some of the things that we were doing that were not traditional were helping the Afghan government develop its capacity to better communicate with the Afghan people.

That capacity had been shattered over many decades of conflict and so rebuilding that, not just in terms of material, but people— training spokespersons, training people how to be effective communicators, training people within the government how to get a message out, how to explain themselves to their people—that was a key—a key goal of ours, that—and we were not front and center. We tried to, as much as we could, help the Afghan government at all levels—you know, local, national, you know, provincial— to better connect with its own citizens and explain their own policies, what they were doing, why they were doing and so forth. So that was something a bit unusual about our operations in Afghanistan.

MR. KELMAN: And just one final question: How do you think we did?

MR. LUSSENHOP: Well, I'm biased since I was there.

MR. KELMAN: (Chuckles.)

MR. LUSSENHOP: I think that there are a lot of untold success stories. I think our public diplomacy and public messaging was very effective. There are huge challenges that are outside the realm of public diplomacy, that are outside of really anyone's control, and I think the main thing is that we focused in on specific objectives where we could fill a niche, where we could achieve something and went for that.

And I think, thanks to our efforts, we had improving English scores; we had better and better applications for Fulbright exchange. We had a huge increase in the use of SMS text messaging as a social networking system, which is something that we set up. And we had a government that went from being very, very incapable of communicating—I mean, the Afghan government—to being pretty effective at getting its message out quickly, especially following crises or security incidents.

So, not to say we didn't have some of our failures as well; I mean, in an environment like that, you're doing a lot, you're working hard, you're trying a lot and not everything works, but you—and especially in a conflict environment, in a really high-priority place like Afghanistan—you have to try new things, you have to take—and you have to take risks and I think, by and large, a lot of our programs were having an effect.

Haynes Mahoney, Counselor for Public Affairs, U.S. Embassy, Cairo, Egypt

Q: Today is July 7, 2011, and the following is an interview with Mr. Haynes Mahoney. Until recently, he was the counselor of public affairs in the U.S. Embassy in Cairo, Egypt. Could you tell us briefly about the nature of your public diplomacy programming in Cairo, before what has been called the Egyptian revolution occurred, that toppled the Mubarak government? Who were your major audiences, and how did you establish a meaningful dialogue with them?

HAYNES MAHONEY: Well, thank you for this opportunity. Our audiences in Egypt—the most important one were the youth. And when I say "the youth" I mean the people that we call traditionally opinion leaders. That's the people that I would characterize as the ones that we engaged directly, whether it was through exchange programs, or whether it was bringing American experts on various topics to Egypt to interact with them, or whether it was bringing musical performing groups, for example, to show them a side of America that they didn't normally get.

The situation we faced in Egypt was, frankly, a big challenge in terms of misperceptions about the United States—who we are as a people and what our intentions are in that region that's experienced colonialism, a lot of invasion and outside manipulation and, frankly, is very worried about the United States as the sole remaining superpower. So our goal was really to make our—the nature of our society better understood, beyond the action films and some American television programs and aspects of pop culture that people were familiar with, but certainly don't represent the whole of the United States.

That was one part of it; the other part of it, of course, was just the action that we had—interaction we had with the news media, which was very important to articulate what was behind our foreign policies. And that reached a broader audience through television and of course new information technology, and got out to a much wider audience of Egyptians. But the young people, for us, were truly critical.

Q: Now that Egypt is seeking to implement democratic reforms, will your successor have to make major changes in the Embassy's approach to communicating with the old and especially new audiences, or greatly alter the content of your programming and exchanges activities?

MR. MAHONEY: I think there are a lot of new opportunities for my successor. I think the basic themes will not change that much. We always tried to support the sense of civil society, a rise in awareness of youthful potential, whether it was through politics or through economic enterprise. We had a model American Congress, for example.

And we had an extremely active alumni organization in Egypt. This—these were people who had been on our exchange programs and when they returned to Egypt, they had seen American society. They—we tried to pair them up in America with their counterparts. So they had a good idea about what civil society can do, even before the revolution. And they organized a lot of seminars, a lot of workshops, career building and so forth, on their own.

And many of these youths were actual participants in the January 25th movement. So when Tahrir Square was going on, when the protests were going on—these massive demonstrations that were organized—we were able to contact them—be in touch with them. We knew these people, many of them quite well. And many of them had been on our programs—on exchange programs that looked at American civil society.

So our goal now is to build on those contacts and that work that we have done over many, many years, and to take advantage of that to—because people in Egypt are looking—they're going to forge their own way. They're going to work their own way through progress towards democracy. But I think, to the extent that they can benefit from our experiences both good and bad, that's just part of the mix that helps them.

Q: This has been an interview with Mr. Haynes Mahoney, former counselor for public affairs in the U.S. Embassy in Cairo, Egypt. Thank you very much.

MR. MAHONEY: Thank you very much.

Rafik Mansour, Cultural Affairs Officer, U.S. Embassy, Paris, France

Q: This video is being recorded in the American Embassy in Paris. Today's date is September 30th, 2011.

My guest today is Mr. Rafik Mansour, cultural affairs officer of the U.S. Embassy in Paris. Mr. Mansour, student and academic exchange programs, along with professional exchange programs, have traditionally made an important contribution to the furtherance of understanding between Americans and citizens of other countries. Does the U.S. Embassy in France have a particular focus in your exchange programs' design or in the selection of candidates for these exchanges? How do you make your programs all-inclusive in a country as diverse as France?

RAFIK MANSOUR: Excellence has always been the main criterion for selection of our participants in the student and professional exchanges. In the current French government, the president, the prime minister and the foreign minister are all alumni of the International Visitor Leadership Program—one of the flagship programs of the State Department. Needless to say, the positive experience they had in the United States on the IVLP while in their 20s and 30s is helping us today advance the bilateral relationship as these officials have now gotten to such leadership positions in their country.

As you pointed out in your question, France is a multicultural society. Ethnic and religious diversity is one of the many things we have in common with the French. It's a source of wealth for both of our countries. France is a very secular country, and we are of course respectful of that in our outreach and programming activities. At the same time, France has the largest Muslim population in Western Europe. It also has the largest Jewish population in Western

Europe. To ignore this would be ignoring an important part of French society—would be ignoring an important part of France.

In his 2009 speech at Cairo University, President Obama pledged a new beginning between the U.S. and Muslims all over the world, based on mutual interest and mutual respect. Here in France, our embassy does not single out any one particular group for outreach. Our goal is to be inclusive and to make sure that no group is ignored. In Embassy France, we are on the lookout for talent and excellence throughout the country, whether it's in the big cities, smaller towns or the French suburbs—"le banlieue," as the French call them—where diversity and unemployment rates are usually higher than in the rest of France.

Today 30 percent of our participants in the International Visitors Leadership Program come from our diversity outreach efforts. The Fulbright Commission is attracting exceptional talent from non- traditional audiences, including for the U.S. Summer Institutes for Young Leaders. And Embassy Paris is running its Youth Ambassador Program, which enables outstanding French high school students, on scholarship, to travel the U.S., meet their peers, development leadership and community service skills, and serve as ambassadors of goodwill, of France and all of its diversity to our country.

Q: Can you provide some examples of a few particularly successful outreach efforts and describe what specific United States foreign policy objective or objectives are being achieved by these efforts?

MR. MANSOUR: Our ambassador has been very successful in getting U.S. star power—Samuel Jackson, Woody Allen, Jodie Foster, will.i.am—to help us with our outreach efforts to the French public in general, and French youth and diversity communities in particular. It has been very impactful for French youth to get to meet such legends, to get to hear about their careers and the hardships that they have had to endure and overcome in order to reach the very top of their industries and get life and career advice from such international figures.

Here at the U.S. Embassy in France, we have been connecting with minority figures at the grassroots level for a number of years. However, in order to ensure that our efforts will have a lasting impact in France, we have taken our outreach to the institutional level. Working with the political section and the foreign commercial service, public affairs has partnered with elite institutions in France, within government but also NGOs, the media, private companies and the Franco-American Fulbright Commission, in order to help us advance and sustain our outreach efforts throughout France.

The result is twofold. First of all, we have succeeded in making the U.S. voice heard and respected about the importance of diversity. And second, partnering with the right French institutions, we have helped hundreds of French underprivileged youth from different backgrounds gain better access as well as better mentoring and networking opportunities that enables them to secure a better position in France's higher education system and the job market, thus reaching maximum potential here in France.

For instance, we have connected French underprivileged high school students, the corporate world, elite high schools, elite universities and their alumni networks in order to help these underprivileged French students better prepare for the very selective entrance examinations, for "les grandes écoles" France's finest institutions of higher learning, get scholarships to go to these schools, and also get the kind of mentoring and networking opportunities needed to ensure not only successful completion of studies but also good jobs upon graduation.

Traditionally, the "grandes écoles" in France were out of reach for these underprivileged youth. And so this is an important step forward in French society. By helping the development of a future generation of French leaders that is representative of all of France's diversity, we are advancing President Obama's vision here in France. A France that is capable of helping all of its citizens reach their full potential is a stronger France, a more powerful leader within Europe and a stronger ally of the United States.

Q: Thank you for your interesting remarks. This interview took place at the U.S. Embassy in Paris on September 30th, 2011.

MR. MANSOUR: Thank you.

Transcripts prepared by Federal News Service, Washington, DC.

Appendix 2. Remarks by Thomas A. Shannon, U.S. Ambassador to Brazil

"The Last Three Feet" Symposium at The George Washington University, November 3, 2011

AMBASSADOR THOMAS SHANNON: Well, good morning. It's a real pleasure to be here. And Bud, thank you very much. If there's anything to take away from Bud's introduction, it's that I have trouble keeping a job. (Laughter.) But it's—again, he is right. I did fly up last night.

And I did so because of Bud but also because of the excellent reputation that George Washington University has and that especially the Public Diplomacy Council and George Washington University's Institute for Public Diplomacy and Global Communication has and because of what for me was the very interesting topic here.

Because in many ways, this is an opportunity to listen to some excellent practitioners talk about the kinds of challenges they have faced in the field and the different techniques and tools they have used to face those challenges, some successfully, some not.

But always in a learning mode, always intent on evolving our public diplomacy and doing so in ways that are not only relevant for the regions in which they are working but more broadly relevant for our larger public diplomacy, our larger diplomatic goals in the world. And in this regard, I think all of you have in store for you a real treat.

My guess is it's going to be very interactive because that's what public diplomacy is. And it's going to be an opportunity not only for the different practitioners and panelists to share their views but also to respond to your questions and listen to your comments. You know, as I was preparing for this talk, I thought that I should talk a little bit about my own experience.

I've spent my career—27 years now—mostly in the Western Hemisphere but also in Africa. I'm what's called a dusty roads diplomat. I'm the kind of person that has always kind of worked in societies that are in transition from one phase of their existence to another.

In the Western Hemisphere and in South Africa, it was largely transitions from authoritarian governments to the democratic governments, from closed economies to open economies, from autarchic societies or countries to countries that were involved in very extensive processes of regional integration and countries that historically had been isolated or marginalized into countries that are playing an increasingly important role on the global stage.

But also countries that are moving beyond democratic governance to creating democratic societies and democratic states, and in the process of doing it, kind of reexamining their own national histories, reexamining their own national interests and reshaping them in ways that are sometimes very helpful to us and sometimes quite unsettling.

And as we—as I have kind of engaged in these societies over time, I've learned a few things. And I wanted to share some of them—some of them with you today.

But as I do so, I'm kind of reminded of a quote from Dean Acheson, who, kind of looking back on the years immediately following World War II and leading into the

Cold War, said at that time the significance of events was shrouded in ambiguity and we hesitated long before grasping what now seems obvious.

It's very commonplace at events like this to talk about the tremendous changes that are taking place in the world, to talk about these tectonic shifts, whether it's in the Middle East or North Africa or South Central Asia or elsewhere, that are releasing these enormous political, economic and social energies and to kind of wring our hands as we attempt to determine how best to deal with these.

And you know, as we sit here and try to figure out how we grasp the obvious, I think it's important to understand that many of the people who will be talking to you today have got their hand on the obvious, have touched the obvious and are building ways to deal with the obvious that are going to help us a lot.

But as I think back on how our public diplomacy has evolved in the Western Hemisphere in particular, there's a couple of things that come to mind immediately. The first is that as we engage in these societies in transition, that increasingly what become the drivers in our relationship are not bilateral issues. They're not this tariff or that tax. They're not what good gets in and what good doesn't get in. These are important.

But they're not the most important things. The real drivers in so much of our larger diplomacy today are global issues and global trends. They are things like food security, energy security, availability of water, public health policies, how the justice ministries and court systems and police systems connect with each other.

And as we—as we kind of fashion not only our state-to-state diplomacy but more broadly our public diplomacy, we need to keep in mind that at the end of the day people are interested in broad trends. People see the broad trends and they understand how those broad trends connect to their daily lives.

They understand what climate change means. They understand what environmental stewardship is. They understand what it means to have access to cheap energy. They understand what it means to have access to good public healthcare.

And they understand the connections that exist between all of the countries as they try to fashion broad regional and hemispheric policies because there's also—as these drivers become global, there's also increasing awareness that the solutions are transnational or multilateral.

And this is where public diplomacy can play such an important role because first of all it's about making our diplomacy public. It's about explaining our diplomacy, explaining our actions as a nation in a larger world to other people. But it's more than that really.

It's not just a public relations campaign or an ad campaign because as we explain our diplomacy, what we're really doing is promoting diplomacy between publics. We're really promoting diplomacy between societies and looking for those connecting points between societies that are going to show that we are somehow relevant, that we are somehow meaningful to the kinds of challenges and issues that the countries in the world are facing today.

And as I look back on my experience in the Western Hemisphere, and most recently in Brazil, what's striking for me is as societies connect, the social becomes more important. This does not mean the politics and economics slide away. They're still very important, as are security issues and other issues of traditional diplomacy.

But the emergence of the social, the emergence of the fight against poverty, the fight against inequality, the fight against social exclusion and the effort to fashion through our democratic political systems and through our market economies some kind of social justice, some kind of system that responds to the aspirations of people. And that recognizes that individuals want not only a voice in determining their national destinies but a voice in determining their individual destinies, and the opportunities and the tools to achieve those individual destinies becomes a very important aspect of how we engage with each other.

And in this regard, I think that public diplomacy, and especially the practitioners of public diplomacy, are really in many ways at the forefront of our engagement in the world. If they were miners, we would say they're at the rock face, chipping away every day at a reality that is constantly changing and is constantly challenging and sometimes quite dangerous.

But as we think about, you know, how we engage, it becomes, I think, increasingly apparent that we have to show people, societies and countries that we can help them succeed and that their success is best achieved through democratic systems of government, through open societies and free market economies that connect regionally and globally. And there are varieties of ways to do this obviously.

And some of this is an effort of kind of test and see what works and test and see what doesn't work and then adapt over time.

But for instance, as we look at the country I'm at right now, Brazil, when President Obama visited Brazil in March of this year and met with President Rousseff, it was a historic meeting in the sense that it was the first African-American president meeting the first female Brazilian president and engaging in a discussion that was really going to define a 21st century agenda in the U.S.-Brazil relationship.

And as the two engaged over the course of the day, it became apparent that their agenda was strikingly different from what that agenda might have looked like in the past. They identified four priorities that were both national priorities and bilateral priorities. And those were infrastructure development, advancements in science and technology, education and innovation.

From our point of view, all four of those are essential for us—the United States—to maintain a leading role in the world and to continue to have an economy that produces that kinds of jobs and income that our citizens demand. For Brazil, these four areas were absolutely essential to its national development and for Brazil to accomplish the last three feet of its economic, political and social development, as it moves to becoming a fully developed society.

This is a country, in case you don't know, which has in a very short period of time pushed about 30 million people out of extreme poverty and created a middle class of about a hundred million people which is more than half of Brazil.

So a country that historically had been defined by its inequalities increasingly defined by its middle-class nature, but a middle class that is a consumer-based middle class much like the United States and which wants all of the things that the United States middle class wants.

And as the two leaders kind of looked for ways to implement or give some content or substance to this vision of theirs, this 21st century vision, they focused on things like tying together our ethnic and racial histories of diversity.

We have something called the joint action plan against ethnic and racial discrimination that links together Brazilian civil society and American civil society to exchange our practices and those that are good and those that are bad on what have helped us build a larger, more open society, more diverse society.

We've signed a memorandum of understanding on the advancement of women and girls, with special focus not only on fighting violence against women and girls but also promoting their empowerment through education and opening up economic opportunities and building special programs that link female scientists in the United States and in Brazil to enhance the attractiveness of the study of mathematics and science and engineering in Brazil and in the United States.

We have worked together on programs—public-private partnerships that have brought American companies together to fashion larger strategic initiatives that those American companies can pursue that clearly show a commitment to Brazil's success.

And in this regard it's about American companies funding English-language training programs in the favelas of Rio in anticipation of the World Cup in 2014 and the Olympics in 2016, the recognition being that English-language training is not a cultural tool. It's a social and economic tool that allows people to get jobs, especially in service sectors that are going to have to respond to a variety of visitors from around the world, all of whom will be speaking English in one form or another as their language of communication inside of Brazil.

It has to do with fashioning an agreement on cooperation and space, which might sound odd with a country like Brazil but Brazil does have a space program, it does have a launch site which has the unique capability of launching along the equator, very attractive for people who want to put satellites into space.

And as Brazil builds that launch site, it is a launch site that carries with it not just commercial advantage but enormous practical advantage to Brazilian society because through certain kinds of global precipitation measurement programs and other from-space observation programs, Brazil will be able to anticipate the kind of flooding and mudslides that killed thousands of people in the state of Rio de Janeiro and Pernambuco a year ago.

And also we've built an open skies agreement that will allow Brazilian and U.S. airlines to fly back and forth with enormous frequency, addressing the huge surge in demand for non- immigrant visas, for tourist and visitor visas that we're experiencing in Brazil these days. And this—Brazil right now is the third largest country in the world in terms of receipt of nonimmigrant visas.

This year we're going to authorize over 800,000 visas in Brazil. Next year, it's going to be a million and the next year it's going to be 1.3 million. And Sao Paolo is the largest single visa authorizing post in the world at this point in time. And this, I think, highlights the connectedness between U.S. and Brazilian society and the kind of demand that Brazilians are expressing to travel to the United States.

And so we need to find a way to kind of open up those sluice gates not only in terms of facilitating our visa processes but also in creating the mechanisms to travel. And the reason I've kind of walked through these examples is to highlight that so much of what we're doing in our bilateral relationship is not being driven by what governments want.

It's being driven by what our societies want and how they want to communicate with each other, how they want to connect with each other and how they want our governments to facilitate that process.

And as we—as we think about this, as we think about how we incorporate this social into our societies, into our diplomacy, it's evident that the tool that we're going to use to do this is our public diplomacy because it really is about understanding what's happening on the other side of those three feet, what's happening in the societies that we're operating in, what's happening in the countries that we are operating in.

And that's why I entitled this talk "Reversing Polarity" because the tendency in understanding is to think of public diplomacy as something we emit, as something that we produce in order to convince people to think a certain way. And there is an aspect of that. There is a certain truth to that.

But to be successful in the 21st century, public diplomacy also has to be about responding to what people are saying to us, listening to what they're saying to us and using that information, using that—the insight we get—in order to fashion programs and outreach that connects to those people.

And one of the things that has struck me, for instance, as we engage in public diplomacy in Brazil, is how we are in the process of creating programs in which Brazilians come to us. We don't have to go to them. And the reason Brazilians are coming to us is because there are aspects of the program that are important to them. Some of them will be talked about today.

One is a program called Jovens Embaixadores, which means youth ambassadors, in which we select—this was a public-private partnership originally funded by FedEx. Today it's funded by a much larger constellation of companies in which we send a relatively small group— originally it was 35, this year it was 45—young Brazilians, ages 15 to 17, to the United States for three to four weeks where they are Brazil's ambassadors to the communities that they visit.

And I think you'll be fascinated by the description which is going to be done today. But last year, we just named the latest 45 youth ambassadors and we have 7,500 applicants. And again, in a country of 200 million, that might seem like small beer. But actually, this is something that has grown quite dramatically over time and if we had more money, we could send a lot more people to the United States.

But what's striking is that within Brazilian society and among Brazilian youth, there is a group of young men and young women—15-, 16-, 17-years-old—in public schools who have taught themselves English, who have learned enough about American society and American culture that they want to come to the United States who are doing well in their schools, are doing well in their communities and who are looking for a way to connect with us in a significant way.

And the degree to which we can open that door for them and bring them in, we shape their attitudes towards us. We shape their attitudes towards themselves. And we help to build a future cadre of leadership at the community, local, state and national level which is going to be very open to us.

Now, this might sound a lot like the old international visitors program. And in some ways it is. But the difference is in the international visitors program, we went out looking for people. We tried to pick who the leaders were going to be. Here, we're letting them come to us and I think that's a better strategy because leaders are self-selected. They're not chosen by others.

And the extent to which we can take these kinds of programs and expand them and use them to pull people in, they're going to be very useful to us. I also—I mentioned the English- language programs that we're doing today. And as I noted, these really aren't cultural programs, at least not in how they're perceived. They really are social and economic tools for advancement.

And as we work with our binational and bicultural centers around Brazil, as we work with our private sector, we've found an enormous desire to connect with us in the area of English language training that is going to be I think central to our larger diplomacy as we move forward because it's going to make Brazil an anchor point for English language training throughout South America and the country that is going to be a reference point for people who speak English as a second language.

And in this regard during the president's visit we also signed a memorandum of understanding—a little bit of what we called mega events which is really about the World Cup and the Olympics and how we create an umbrella structure and dialogue in the area of security, public health and larger management of large events that will allow the Brazilians to successfully conduct the World Cup and the Olympics.

And our English language training, as I mentioned, kind of connects very nicely to this broader project because it's all about us committing to Brazil's success and committing to

Brazil's success in a way that responds to our own national interests and to our own needs of a safe game, not only for American athletes but also for American tourists.

But as we think about Brazil, as I think about the Western Hemisphere, it really does strike me that we are at a moment in time in which, as important as states are, as important as countries are, what is really going to determine our status in the hemisphere and our wellbeing in our hemisphere is how our societies connect.

And we are going to play a central role in facilitating that connection if we're smart. And I think we are. And I think the secretary and the president have made important strides in this area. And I think a lot of this is going to come clear as you listen to the practitioners today. And I don't pretend that the lessons from the Western Hemisphere are somehow applicable easily throughout the world.

There are lots of differences in this world and programs need to be fashioned and managed to be responsive to the publics that we are dealing with. But I do think there are a couple of underlying lessons that are important. The first is we have to be relevant to people in order to be successful. We are no longer in a world in which there are ideological defaults that people—that require people to go one way or another almost automatically.

On a daily basis in our diplomacy, we have to show to the countries we are operating in that we are relevant to their success and we have to show to the citizens of those countries that we are relevant not only to their success but to their happiness and to their ability to fulfill themselves as individuals. And that means more than opportunities. It means more than economic opportunities. It means tools.

It means we need to be able to show that we are helping empower them in some way, either through education or through providing the right kind of health care of helping to create the right kind of security environment for their families and there's a lot we can do here. And there's a lot we can do in the area of cooperation. And it's not all about money. It's not all about budgets.

It's really about coordination. It's about working through transnational and multilateral institutions but also working through our own civil societies and connecting our civil societies.

I also think that, you know, aside from looking for ways to be relevant in the countries we operate in and looking for ways to be relevant in the societies we're operating in and aside from looking for ways to empower people, this is also about recognizing that at the end of the day diplomacy is an act of accommodation.

It's an act of understanding and empathy that allows us to find those points on which we can agree. Points in which we can disagree are obvious in many instances and manifold. But the trick is to highlight that we do have an ability to understand each other, that we do have an ability to connect and build off those connections in a positive way.

And in this regard, I want to close by recalling an article that Secretary of State Elihu Root wrote in the very first issue of Foreign Affairs magazine in 1922. This is an article that was called "Requisites for Success of Popular Diplomacy," an appropriate title for today.

You might recall in the aftermath of World War I, a lot of people were trying to figure out what went wrong in diplomacy and what allowed an international system to collapse into the kind of warfare that was World War I.

And there was great anxiety especially among diplomats about the emergence of new nations and new democracies and what that was going to mean for diplomacy and in particular what that was going to mean for the ability of states to communicate with each other and connect with each other. And Root wrote that when foreign affairs were ruled by autarchies, by monarchs or oligarchies, the danger of war was in sinister purpose. When foreign affairs are ruled by democracies, the danger of war will be in mistaken beliefs.

That was very prescient given what happens with World War II. But as he got deeper into the subject, he referred to public diplomacy as a kind of education. He said public opinion will be increasingly not nearly the ultimate judge but an immediate and active force in negotiation.

And he described the purpose of diplomacy as being to rescue from the field of difference and controversy and transfer to the field of common understanding and agreement one subject after another. And that diplomacy in itself is the history—the long history — of the process of adjustment between different ideas and of the prejudices and passions and hitherto irreconcilable differences, which had baffled adjustment.

As Root kind of thought about the impact of our societies in our world, he recognized that as diplomats, we needed to find ways to enhance understanding, enhance empathy, find points of agreement and look for ways to connect those points of agreement so that we can find common purpose.

And in this regard, public diplomacy really becomes a space where our values and our interests intersect and where we display them to others and get them to show us their values and interests and look for ways that based on that we can build common action on behalf of our citizens.

And in that regard, I would like to congratulate George Washington University and the Public Diplomacy Council for this event. I would like to congratulate the panelists for their role in describing what I think are important advances in our public diplomacy. I would like to thank all of you for being here today in what I think is going to be understood as a seminal event in understanding what we're doing and what more we need to be doing.

But I'll close by saying that the history of the 20th century was a history of war. It was a history of national ambition and technological and industrial advance conflicting with international structures and diplomatic capacities that weren't up to the struggle. As we look into the 21st century, I don't think we're going to see that kind of warfare.

But I do think that the conflict that we are going to face is going to be a conflict that is going to be fought out not kinetically but—that's a euphemism—not kinetically, not on the field of battle but in the imaginations of our cultures and the social accomplishments of our countries. So again, thank you very much for your time. Thank you for your patience. It's been a real pleasure. (Applause.)

Transcript by Federal News Service, Washington, DC.

Appendix 3. An Interview with Michelle Kwan, U.S. Public Diplomacy Envoy

Q: This interview was conducted on September 21st, 2011, at George Washington University, and will be included in the forum on The Last Three Feet—New Activities, New Media, and New Challenges for American Public Diplomacy. The forum is hosted by the Institute of Public Diplomacy and Global Communication in George Washington University and the Public Diplomacy Council.

Michelle Kwan's skills and ambitions took her to many parts of the world at an early age. Her talent, grace, friendly manner and hard work earned her both championships and millions of fans around the world. Since November, 2006, Ms. Kwan has truly become a world citizen whose travels as a State Department American public diplomacy envoy have involved explaining American society, values, traditions, to students and athletes and others—from China to Argentina, from Korea to Russia.

She has notable achievements: In ice skating, winning 43 championships including five world championships; she's a member of the President's Council on Fitness, Sport and Nutrition; and as a student with a BA in international studies from the University of Denver and an MA in international relations from the Fletcher's Law—School of Law and Diplomacy at Tuffs University. Michelle, welcome.

MICHELLE KWAN: Thank you.

Q: Michelle, Secretary Condoleezza Rice in 2005 named you as an American sports—American public diplomacy envoy. Can you tell us a little bit about your exact duties and the—some—the audiences you've met and what you've told them about the United States—its people and its values and institutions?

MS. KWAN: Well, since 2006, when I was appointed, I've had some amazing travels all over the world, like you said—Argentina, Russia, Ukraine, Singapore—met amazing people. And I guess, as a public diplomacy envoy, I have a couple of goals. First is to have a positive influence, to be able to share my story, the things that I have learned through sports like hard work, dedication, focus—falling, sometimes, on the ice—(chuckles)—and getting back up. And these are universal concepts—and I hope that these students can apply into their own lives.

And, I guess, second is, by that interaction, by having a dialogue—a conversation, not a monologue—that we can learn about each other. Hopefully they can learn about America—the U.S.—and sometimes they have misconceptions about the United States. Sometimes they think of the U.S. and they think of Hollywood or they think of New York, they think of—and sometimes even bad misconceptions that I might be able to answer some of the questions that they might have.

And also it's a chance for me to learn. I've traveled a lot of countries through sports, through skating. But now, as an envoy, I get to learn and interact with people and learn about people from different cultures, different values, different traditions. And so it's just been an incredible experience.

Q: In your travels abroad you've been supported by U.S. Foreign Service officers and their assistants who are citizens of that host country. I wonder if you could share an anecdote or two of some of the experiences you've had with these Foreign Service officers either in briefing you or attending one of your programs.

MS. KWAN: The Foreign Service officers and the public affairs officers that I have met abroad are truly remarkable. They do an extraordinary job at representing our country abroad. They have language skills, they know the people that they interact with, and they're so prepared. I've had amazing experiences, even through my trips as an envoy, where they put together briefing books that are about this big.

And I'm going, this is—it's only a week-and-a-half trip, and yet there are pages on everything from the size, the population, the food that people enjoy at that specific country, then more specifically, the people I'm going to meet throughout my trip. And then, of course, there is usually a bit—a few hours of downtime where, like in Argentina, they scheduled an hour and a half of tango because to experience the Argentine culture you have to have tango in there. So it's incredible. They do an amazing job.

Q: You've traveled officially to China, Russia, Korea, Ukraine, Singapore, other places. These are very different societies; and I wonder what your impressions were of the people you met with, especially the students, and what sort of serious or humorous questions did some of the students throw your way?

MS. KWAN: Wow. (Chuckles.) I've had so many different questions from students and government officials. From students I've had—a few in Russia—it was a very, very smart question. Says: Do Americans think that in Russia there's bears running around? See, sometimes it goes both ways. Sometimes American students might have misconceptions of Russian—of Russia. And I said, well, maybe, but I will help them understand, hopefully if I get a chance to meet these Americans, that Russia is—there's not bears running around.

But also I asked, well, what do you think the U.S. is like? And she's like, well, taxi cabs, lights, buildings—kind of the image of New York. And I said, well, yes, maybe in New York, but you might have the countryside in other parts of the U.S. You might have California, Colorado—the mountains. You have other parts of the U.S. that I try to describe to them, because I might be the first American that they ever meet. So it's important to be able to answer some of the questions that they might have—they're curious minds.

And I also encourage them to learn more about the U.S. and to even learn English and travel—and not just the U.S., but in Japan and Russia, learn about people from other cultures because the world is getting smaller. I said, what happens if one day you'll be working closely with people in the U.S., working closely with people in Japan, working closely with people in Korea? You have to have that understanding. And the better the understanding, the better the relationship will be.

Q: Based on your international experiences in meeting with diverse groups of people, do you have any recommendations or suggestions for those who will be in our forum audience as students about what they should consider if they're thinking about a career in international affairs—be it in the private sector or with the U.S. government?

MS. KWAN: I think my advice is: follow your passion. I think having a curious mind is important, whether it be in the private sector or in the public sector. If you're a Foreign Service officer you have to be adventurous to go from one country to another country to another country every few years.

And I think even in the private sector, there are times when you jump from one country to another or you work directly for one country and then another country.

So a curious mind in the sense that—having an understanding with the people that you work with overseas, having the understanding in sort of a broad scope, where they come from—cultural understanding, and also similarities. And I think that's what it's all about. It's all about building relationships from people to people, country to country. And I think that's essentially what, to me, my idea of public diplomacy is—building that strong foundation, that friendship.

Q: Finally, when you're not doing your envoy travels, what sort of things are you involved in now? I know that you have come to Washington as a base for at least this time period. And I'm wondering if you could talk to us about some of the other activities you're involved in?

MS. KWAN: Well, since I finished skating competitively— I have that sort of curious mind where I continued my education—I finished at the University of Denver, then I continued to get my master's at the Fletcher School of Law and Diplomacy, where I focused on foreign policy analysis. And now I made the move to Washington, DC, and have continued to travel as a public diplomacy envoy—and working with the President's Council on Fitness, Sports and Nutrition. I'm also doing something with U.S. Woman China LEAD—which is focused on U.S. and—U.S.-China.

So it's always wanting to learn, wanting to expand my experiences and my knowledge. And, I guess, continue on that path. A lot of people wonder—how did you go from figure skating to diplomacy? And they can't see that connection. But I can tell you that the experiences that I have gained through skating and traveling all over the world—it's really opened my eyes, trying to understand. And now through school and perhaps even a PhD—I'm kind of flirting with the idea of a PhD—just having that idea of wanting to learn and wanting to understand. (Chuckles.)

Q: I—one other question, if I might. Your parents, I believe, came from China. And you went there as an envoy. Did that particular trip have a great significance for you?

MS. KWAN: I've traveled to China many, many times, and to Hong Kong. My parents are from Hong Kong and I speak Cantonese at home. And growing up Chinese-American—I feel it was very, very special to me, because I grew up understanding the Chinese culture—celebrating Chinese New Year, my family owned a Chinese restaurant, speaking Cantonese at home.

But then, at the same time, I'm born and raised USA—American. So when I travel to China it was—as an envoy, it was definitely an amazing experience to see it and to say, oh, wow, I'm representing the U.S. going to China. And I just—I felt, wow, this is—my parents, when they immigrated to the United States, it's the land of the golden opportunity. And I think when I went to China I was like, wow, everything—my parents' dream came true.

Q: Very good. Well, we thank you for your time and your interest in our program, and wish you luck in your future experiences as an American public diplomacy envoy. Thank you very much.

MS. KWAN: Thank you.

Transcript by Federal News Service, Washington, DC.

Appendix 4. Navigating the Acronym Maze

The State Department can hardly match the U.S. military for arcane and short-handed terminology. Still public diplomacy does have its own set of abbreviations and acronyms. Here is a sampling.

AC	American Center
ACAO	Assistant Cultural Affairs Officer
AIO	Assistant Information Officer
Alhurra TV	Arabic news and information television
america.gov	Former IIP Web site for international audiences, now archived
APAO	Assistant Public Affairs Officer
BBG	Broadcasting Board of Governors
BNCs	Binational Centers
CAO	Cultural Affairs Officer
DCM	Deputy Chief of Mission
DPAO	Deputy Public Affairs Officer
ECA	Bureau of Educational and Cultural Affairs
eJournals	IIP electronic (Web-based) publications
ELF	English Language Fellow
ETA	English Teaching Assistant
ETF	English Teaching Forum
FSB	Fulbright Scholarship Board
FSN	Foreign Service National Employee, aka LES

FSO	Foreign Service Officer
IBB	International Broadcasting Board
IIE	Institute for International Education
IIP	Bureau of International Information Programs
iipdigital	Current IIP Web site providing materials to U.S. embassies and missions (iipdigital.usembassy.gov)
IO	Information Officer aka Press Attaché
IRC	Information Resource Center
IRO	Information Resource Officer
IVLP	International Visitor Leadership Program
J-1 Visa	Visa to participate in State Department exchange program
LES	Locally Employed Staff
MBN	Middle East Broadcasting Network (Sawa/Alhurra
PA	Bureau of Public Affairs
PAS	Public Affairs Section
PAO	Public Affairs Officer
PD	Public Diplomacy
PDO	Public Diplomacy Officer
R	Office of the Under Secretary for Public Diplomacy and Public Affairs
Radio Marti	Broadcasting to Cuba
Radio Sawa	Arabic broadcasting for younger audiences with emphasis on pop music
RELO	Regional English Language Officer

RFE/RL	Radio Free Europe/Radio Liberty
RFA	Radio Free Asia
RSS	Real Simple Syndication
USIA	United States Information Agency (1953–1999)
USIS	United States Information Service (USIA overseas)
VOA	Voice of America
YES	Youth Exchange and Study

Contributor Biographies

Dr. Michael Anderson was a member of the Foreign Service for almost 30 years, serving in Indonesia, the Philippines, Singapore, Pakistan and Papua New Guinea. He is currently outreach coordinator for the Third Round of the China–U.S. Strategic and Economic Dialogue. Prior to the Foreign Service, Dr. Anderson worked as an instructor in journalism at the University of Minnesota, a journalist in Minneapolis–St. Paul, an information officer with UNICEF at UN Headquarters in New York, and a Peace Corps Volunteer in Malaysia. He has a PhD in political science from the University of Hawaii/East–West Center, and an MA and BA in Journalism/Mass Communication from the University of Minnesota.

Gloria Berbena is the public affairs officer at the U.S. Interests Section in Havana, Cuba. She joined the Foreign Service in 1989. Her other public diplomacy postings have included tours in Thailand, Italy, and the United States. She is a native Californian and a graduate in political science of the University of California at Davis.

Ambassador John Beyrle was the U.S. ambassador to the Russian Federation in 2011. A career officer in the Senior Foreign Service, Ambassador Beyrle has held policy positions and foreign assignments with an emphasis on U.S. relations with Central and Eastern Europe, Russia, and the USSR since joining the State Department in 1983. Ambassador Beyrle's overseas service has included two previous tours at the U.S. Embassy in Moscow, including as deputy chief of mission. He also served as ambassador to Bulgaria. Other overseas assignments include counselor for political and economic affairs at the U.S. Embassy in the Czech Republic, and member of the U.S. delegation to the

CFE Negotiations in Vienna. Washington assignments include acting special adviser to the secretary of state for the New Independent States, and director for Russian, Ukrainian, and Eurasian affairs at the National Security Council. Ambassador Beyrle received a BA with honors from Grand Valley State University, and an MS as a distinguished graduate of the National War College. In 2008, the American University in Bulgaria awarded him a doctoral degree honoris causa.

Beatrice Camp is currently on a State Department detail to the Smithsonian Institution as senior advisor to the under secretary for history, art and culture, after heading the U.S. Consulate General in Shanghai. She has also served overseas in Thailand, Hungary, and Sweden. In Washington, Ms. Camp managed international information programs for Europe, coordinated educational exchange and advising programs worldwide. Before joining the Foreign Service she worked as a reporter and editor in Washington, DC, and New York City and taught English at Chiang Mai University on a fellowship from Oberlin College's Shansi Association.

Walter Douglas is currently at the Center for Strategic and International Studies after serving as minister counselor for public affairs in Pakistan. His overseas assignments include Saudi Arabia, Turkey, Cyprus, Iceland, South Korea, and the Ivory Coast. He worked as executive assistant to the under secretary for public diplomacy and public affairs; director of the Office of Press and Public Diplomacy in the Near Eastern Affairs Bureau at State; and as deputy to the spokesperson at the U.S. Mission to the United Nations. Before joining the Foreign Service, Mr. Douglas worked as an advertising executive in New York and as a legislative assistant in the U.S. House of Representatives. He has a BA in history from the University of Pennsylvania.

Atim Eneida George is a career senior Foreign Service officer with over 25 years of experience in international affairs. She has worked on human rights and democratization, environment, science and technology issues as well as strategic communications. Ms. George holds a BA in speech communications from Boston College, an MA in education from Rutgers University, and an MA in transpersonal psychology from the Institute of Transpersonal Psychology. She received an honorary doctorate from Babcock University for her work in diplomacy and peace initiatives.

Morris E. "Bud" Jacobs is the president of the Public Diplomacy Council, a nonprofit organization dedicated to the academic study, professional practice, and responsible advocacy of public diplomacy. Bud has enjoyed a successful career in business, the nonprofit world, and government. Bud was a consultant to three successive under secretaries for Public Diplomacy and Public Affairs, where he specialized in issues related to U.S. government international broadcasting, Western Hemisphere affairs, and U.S.-Russian relations. Bud was the vice president of the National Council for Eurasian and East European Research. At the Department of State and U.S. Information Agency, Bud held several public diplomacy and policy positions in the USSR, Central and South America, and Washington, DC, and served in political-military positions, including as political advisor to the U.S. Southern Command and special advisor for Bosnian implementation at State and the European Command headquarters in Stuttgart. A native of Colorado, Bud served in the U.S. Army and holds a B.A. with highest honors in Russian and Soviet Studies from the University of California, Santa Barbara. He attended Leningrad State University on a Ford Foundation grant.

Gabriel Kaypaghian is the public diplomacy advisor for Mexico and Canada in the Bureau of Western Hemisphere Affairs at the Department of State. He joined the Foreign Service in 2000 and has served in Mexico City, Rome, Tunis, Guadalajara, and Washington, DC. He previously worked in education as a teacher and school administrator in international schools in Mexico. Mr. Kaypaghian holds a MEd degree from Stanford University and a BS in Foreign Service from Georgetown University.

Dr. William P. Kiehl is editor emeritus of *American Diplomacy* and currently serves as the journal's contributing editor (books). Following a 33-year Foreign Service career in public diplomacy in Europe and Asia, he founded the international public affairs consultancy PDWorldwide in 2003. With State and USIA, he served as principal deputy assistant secretary for educational and cultural affairs, as diplomat in residence at the U.S. Army War College, as PAO in Bangkok, Helsinki, and Prague and in other capacities in Belgrade, Zagreb, Vienna, Colombo, Moscow, and London. His doctorate in higher education management is from the University of Pennsylvania. He is the author of *Global Intentions Local Results*, editor of *America's Dialogue with the World* and *The Eagle and the Elephant: Thai-American Relations Since 1833* and has written a number of articles and book chapters on public diplomacy and international affairs. Dr. Kiehl undertakes special assignments abroad for the Department of State, and lectures at U.S. and international universities on Public Diplomacy. He is a former executive director and the current treasurer of the Public Diplomacy Council.

Michelle Kwan is the most decorated figure skater in U.S. history. Her 43 championships include five world championships, nine U.S. national championships and two Olympic medals in 1998 and 2002. In November 2006, the

U.S. secretary of state appointed Ms. Kwan the first U.S. Public Diplomacy Envoy. In June 2010, President Obama appointed her to the President's Council on Fitness, Sports, and Nutrition, and in December 2010, she was elected to the board of directors of Special Olympics International. Ms. Kwan graduated from the University of Denver with a degree in international studies; earned a master's degree in international relations from the Fletcher School of Law and Diplomacy at Tufts University; and received an honorary doctor of humane letters from Southern Vermont College.

Rachel Graaf Leslie most recently served as the public affairs officer at the U.S. Embassy in Manama, Bahrain. Her previous assignments include Saudi Arabia and Syria. Prior to joining the Foreign Service, Ms. Leslie worked as a program manager at the Institute for International Education. She also studied Middle East politics on a Rotary scholarship at the American University in Cairo. Ms. Leslie holds a BA in political science from Iowa State University and an MPP from the University of Maryland. She is currently on leave from the State Department pursuing a degree in religious studies at the University of Chicago.

Matt Lussenhop is the director of policy and evaluation for the Bureau of Educational and Cultural Affairs, overseeing policy coordination, alumni affairs, program evaluation, and the Cultural Heritage Center. His most recent assignment was public affairs counselor at the U.S. Embassy in Kabul. Prior to that, he served as director of public diplomacy training at the Foreign Service Institute. He has served as a public affairs officer in Sofia, Bulgaria, and Muscat, Oman, and as information officer in Manila, Philippines, and Rabat, Morocco. Other assignments include assistant PAO in Kuwait, assistant CAO in Riyadh, Saudi Arabia, and Arab media officer in NEA/PPD.

Haynes Mahoney is the deputy chief of mission at the U.S. Embassy in Syria. Prior to Damascus, he served as the counselor for press and culture at the U.S. Embassy in Cairo and in Amman and was the cultural attaché in the U.S. Embassy in Cairo. He has also served in Pakistan, Yemen, Germany, and in Syria as a cultural affairs officer at the American Cultural Center in Damascus. He has an MJ from Temple University, an MA in law and diplomacy from the Fletcher School at Tufts University, and a BA from Johns Hopkins University in German literature.

Jean A. Manes is the director for resources for the under secretary for public diplomacy and public affairs. With over 19 years with the State Department, she has served in a variety of public diplomacy positions and as principal officer in the Azores. As cultural affairs officer in Brazil she focused on the utilization of the 38 Binational Centers in the country and the development of a six-year English teaching strategy in advance of the World Cup and Olympic Games in Brazil. She has a master's degree in international management from The American University.

Rafik Mansour is the cultural affairs officer at the U.S. Embassy in Paris. He has also served in Iraq, Algeria, Libya, Russia, Italy, and Haiti. As the CAO in Iraq, Mr. Mansour oversaw the largest Fulbright Foreign Student program in the Middle East and the largest International Visitor Leadership Program in the world. He also served as the political/economic officer at the U.S. Consulate General in St. Petersburg, Russia, and in the political section in Rome. He began his diplomatic career as vice consul in Haiti. Mansour holds a BA in French Literature and a BS in Biology from the University of California-Irvine.

Elizabeth McKay is director of the Office of Press and Public Diplomacy in the Bureau of European and Eurasian

Affairs at the Department of State. She leads the office that supports 49 U.S. Embassies in Europe with their public engagement efforts. Ms. McKay joined the Foreign Service in 1985 and has served in public diplomacy positions in India, Thailand, Laos, and Costa Rica. She was the director for Narcotics and Law Enforcement Affairs at the U.S. Mission to Mexico from 2000 to 2002. Subsequently she served as the deputy director for the Bureau of International Narcotics and Law Enforcement's Office of Africa, Asia, and Europe. Her most recent overseas assignment was as cultural affairs officer at the U.S. Embassy in Ankara. She is a graduate of the National War College and holds the rank of Minister-Counselor. Her languages are Thai, Lao, Spanish, and Turkish. She is married to a Foreign Service officer and has two children.

Ambassador Thomas Shannon is currently the U.S. ambassador to Brazil. Prior to Brazil he was assistant secretary of state for Western hemisphere affairs, special assistant to the president and senior director for Western hemisphere affairs at the National Security Council, and deputy assistant secretary of Western hemisphere affairs at the Department of State. He was also the U.S. deputy permanent representative to the Organization of American States, director for inter-American affairs at the National Security Council, political counselor at the U.S. Embassy in Caracas, Venezuela, and as regional labor attaché at the U.S. consulate general in Johannesburg, South Africa. Ambassador Shannon graduated with high honors from the College of William and Mary. He then studied at Oxford University, where he received DPhil in Politics.

Bruce Wharton is the deputy assistant secretary of state for public diplomacy, Bureau of African Affairs, following service as the director of the Office of Public Diplomacy and Public Affairs and deputy coordinator of the Bureau of

International Information Programs. Mr. Wharton also served as deputy chief of mission at the U.S. Embassy in Guatemala, and on assignments in Argentina, Chile, Bolivia, South Africa, Zimbabwe, and Guatemala. In Africa, he has also had temporary duty in Tanzania, Nigeria, Kenya, and Ghana. He is a graduate of the University of Texas in Austin. Prior to joining the Foreign Service, he worked in professional theater in the Washington, DC, area.

For additional information on Public Diplomacy please consult the Public Diplomacy Council's Web site at:

http://www.publicdiplomacycouncil.org

39360327R00118